LANDMARK VISITORS GUIDE

Dartmoor

Richard Sale

A research scientist before concentrating on travel
writing and photography, Richard's titles for Landmark
include the Côte d'Azur, Cotswolds, Dorset, Italian Lakes,
Madeira, Provence and Somerset.

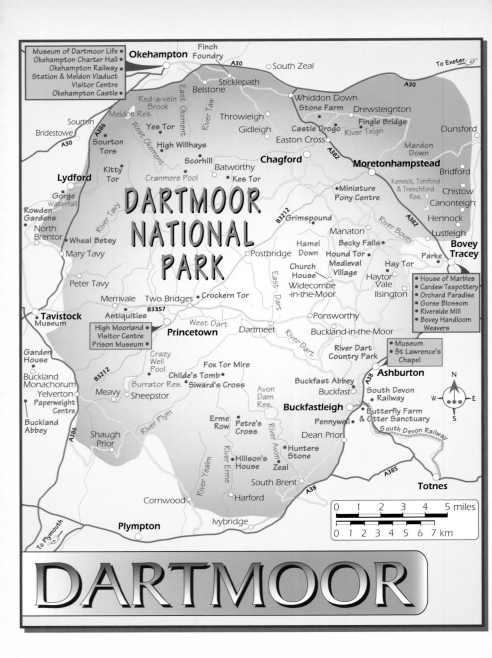

DARTMOOR

Opposite page: Buckfast Abbey, near Buckfastleigh

Dartmoor

Richard Sale

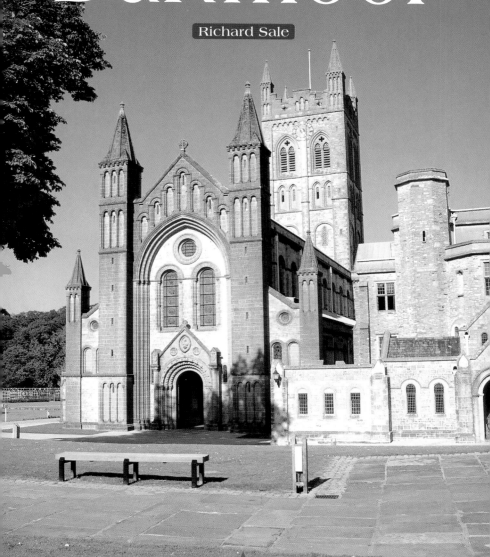

CONTENTS

Left: Morwellham

**Opposite page: The western
end of Castle Drogo**

Introduction

For holidaymakers to the South-West Peninsula, the north and south coasts of Devon are a particular favourite. The coasts are separated by a marvellous pastoral lowland – farms set on red soil, pretty villages and cream teas, and at its heart the vast dome of Dartmoor, one of the finest moors in Britain, a land of uncompromising beauty.

So singular is the Dartmoor landscape that it was made a National Park in 1951. The first-time visitor usually expects to find it clad with purple heather, or dotted with quaint villages such as the Widecombe of Uncle Tom Cobley and all, or covered with the leg-devouring bogs of the Grimpen Mire which confronted Sherlock Holmes in *The Hound of the Baskervilles*. Each of these pictures is, of course, a clichéd view, but, as with all clichés, there is truth behind the stereotype.

Visitors following one of the roads that bisect the moor may glimpse all these aspects, but may also be astonished at the number of other Dartmoors that can be seen – the farmland and luxuriously wooded valleys at the moorland rim, the beautiful rivers, the tors and litter of granite blocks on the hillsides. Because of this diversity the moor has been divided into six areas for the purposes of this book. The northern moor has the highest ground with distinct peaks separated by ground that is often boggy. This is covered by Chapter 1, though Chapter 2 covers a small section of the northern moor as well as an often-forgotten outlying section of lower moorland. The eastern moor is the most 'user-friendly' and has some of the best known beauty spots: this area is covered in Chapter 3. The central moor, that area around Princetown, is covered in Chapter 4. The southern moor is the real wilderness with few landmarks, an occasionally difficult, but rewarding, ground for the walker. This area is covered in Chapters 5 and 6.

All aspects of the moor are considered and some sites outside the National Park are visited. The chapters include some suggestions for walking on the moor: further information on walking, and particularly on the northern moor's military ranges and the restrictions they impose on the walker, can be found in the FactFile at the end of the book. The FactFile also includes other useful information on recreation, accommodation etc.

GRANITE, THE ROCK BENEATH THE MOOR

Around 300 million years ago, the curiously, but exquisitely, named Variscan Orogony (an example of a geological squeezing caused by plate tectonics) created the Cornubian Mountains along the length of what is now the South-West Peninsula. Into the roots of these mountains poured volcanic magma. When the softer, overlying mountains had eroded away, this magma formed a series of six granite masses. Of these, the largest is Dartmoor.

The geologist recognises several forms of granite on Dartmoor, the forms being dependent on how fast the molten magma cooled to form the rock. The fastest cooling creates a coarse-grained rock with deep fissures which weathering turns into the fantastic tors that are such a marvellous feature of Dartmoor. It is an irony that only the existence of an easy-to-reach, finer-grained rock saved the tors for today's walker. Had the fine-grained rock not been so easily quarried, the eighteenth-century quarrymen would have destroyed the tors long before they became a target for those with the leisure time to seek them out.

Granite is essentially composed of three minerals – quartz, feldspar and mica. Quartz in its purest form is clear and colourless but on Dartmoor quartz crystals are normally milky, or even grey. Feldspar exists in two forms, orthoclase, which is white or even pinkish, and plagioclase which is greyish-white. Mica also comes in several forms, but on Dartmoor the usual form is biotite, grey-black in colour. In addition to the three main minerals Dartmoor granite also has smaller quantities of a black mineral called tourmaline.

As the granite cooled, not only did these mineral crystals form, but metallic ores were created. Tin has been the most commercially important ore to have been worked on Dartmoor, though copper, lead and arsenic have also been mined, and zinc, tungsten, cobalt, uranium and even gold exist in small, non-commercially viable, quantities.

FLORA AND FAUNA

All of Dartmoor's granite types form a thin, acidic soil which supports a limited range of plants and encourages the formation of peat and peat bogs. The bogs are of two forms: blanket bog formed on upland sections of moor and the wetter valley bog formed where slow-moving rivers waterlog the soil. Each has its own range of plants, and Dartmoor represents a significant fraction of the world's remaining blanket bog.

In addition to the importance of the moor for its bogs, it is also an important habitat for birds. It is the southernmost breeding area for golden plover and dunlin, and the Dartford warbler has recently colonised the Park. There are important numbers of certain species of dragonflies and the moor is also the only place in the world where one or two species of lichen thrive.

MAN ON THE MOOR

Though Dartmoor was never glaciated or covered with an ice sheet, its ground was frozen because of the ice sheets to the north. When the sheets shrank, the moorland permafrost melted and trees colonised the area. It is likely that man moved in soon after, flint tools dating from the Mesolithic (Middle Stone) Age having been found which probably date from as early as 8,000BC. From that time man's occupation of the moor has been continuous, though it was several thousand years before he left a permanent reminder of his presence on the landscape.

Stone Age

Neolithic (New Stone Age) man buried his dead in tombs made of large slabs of stone, usually three or four uprights, capped with another flat slab. The tomb was then earthed over to form a long barrow. Over time, and particularly on exposed sites, the earth mound sometimes eroded or blew away, leaving the tomb slabs open to the elements. Such a tomb is known as a cromlech or dolmen, and one of the best in Devon lies within the National Park: Spinster's Rock, which lies to the west of Drewsteignton.

Continued on page 10...

The most distinctive features of Dartmoor are its tors. It comes as a surprise to many that granite can be weathered into such weird shapes. But though granite is mechanically tough (one of nature's densest, hardest rocks) it is surprisingly vulnerable chemically. Rainwater, which is slightly acidic, attacks the minerals that form the granite, breaking down biotite into a red-brown slurry which occasionally stains the rock, and helping to form china clay from feldspar. Quartz is a much more resistant mineral and the gravel that forms in the joints between the granite blocks after the feldspar and biotite disintegrate (a gravel called growan by the locals) is composed mainly of quartz crystals.

Rain is not the only weathering agent of the granite, the freezing and thawing of water can have a major effect. Water expands on freezing producing a local pressure in any constriction, that can be more than a hundred times normal atmospheric pressure. The water freezing in cracks in the rock levers the granite blocks apart. This process continues today during the regular freeze-thaws of winter, but was at its most significant during the ice ages.

The rocks of Haytor rising above the flowering gorse and heather

Above: Memorial cross on the south-west flank of Corndon Tor, north-east of Dartmeet

Below left: The old clapper bridge at Dartmeet

Below right: The Court Gate, Bedford Square, Tavistock

Bronze Age

The Stone Age was followed by the Bronze Age, and Dartmoor has the largest and one of the most important concentrations of remains from this period in Britain. While it is obviously true that the relative poverty of the moor in later ages contributed to the survival of the sites – which in more fertile areas might have been ploughed into oblivion – it is clear that the moor was a valuable asset to Bronze Age man.

All over the moor there are hut circles, the bases of their huts. A circular wall of stones, whose collection would have also cleared the moor of boulders inconvenient to herding or planting, was topped by branches which leaned inwards on to a central, vertical pole. A conical roof was then created by laying animal skins or turf over the branches. The huts were floored with stone slabs as earth floors rapidly turn to mud in wet weather.

There are also many megalithic sites that were built at the same time – standing stones, circles and rows of stones, all clearly erected for some ritual purpose by the moorland folk, a purpose which is poorly understood.

Bronze Age folk buried their dead in stone chambers too, but rather than the elaborate, above ground, tombs of the Neolithic period, these chambers (*kistvaens*) were smaller and placed just below the ground. They were of flat stones, the 'lid' lying at ground level. Inside larger boxes the body would be crouched, but more usually cremated remains were placed in much smaller boxes.

The Celts and the Saxons

Around 1,000BC, the climate of Dartmoor declined and this, together with the increased coverage of blanket bog, made the moor less attractive for both crops and herds. The moor seems to have been deserted by about 500BC, though the moorland fringe, particularly on the eastern side, shows evidence of the next great cultural wave sweeping in from mainland Europe – the iron-using Celts.

Roborough Rocks, near Yelverton

The Celts built forts into which they could retreat when threatened, choosing hilltops that they reinforced with ditches and ramparts. In the Teign Valley, to the north of Moretonhampstead, **Cranbrook Castle** and **Prestonbury Castle** are two such hill forts, the best examples in the National Park. Some experts have suggested that these two forts 'protected' the Teign Valley, the river being an easily utilised route into the area, but that may be to read into the forts much more significance than their builders intended.

Beyond the deserted moor the Celts were eventually absorbed into the Roman empire, but soon reestablished their tribal way of life when the legionnaires went home to confront the barbarians on Rome's doorstep. These tribal conflicts allowed the Saxons to conquer England. In the south-west the Saxons pushed the Celts back into Cornwall. To the Saxons the Celts were *wallas*, foreigners, a name derived from the Velcae tribe the Saxons had fought on mainland Europe. The name is the root of Wales and of Dartmoor's Wallabrook, because when the Saxons reached the river it was Celts they found living there.

With the arrival of the Saxons the settlement of Dartmoor and the moorland fringes was established much as it is now, though Saxon Wessex was harassed by Vikings using the Tamar to attack their western border. Tavistock and Buckfast abbeys were originally founded in Saxon times though it was during the Norman period, the 'great age' of English monasticism, that they flourished. The monks of Buckfast Abbey introduced sheep rearing on the poorer moor soils and cereal production in the more fertile areas, changing the face of the moor and becoming rich in the process. Ultimately, of course, it was the power and wealth of the monasteries that led Henry VIII – frightened of the first and greedy for the second – to dissolve the houses.

Medieval to modern times

In late medieval times, the exploitation of the moor's mineral wealth replaced sheep rearing as the major industry, with tin being the most abundant ore. At first the ore was processed on the moor, crude furnaces producing an impure metal which was pack-horsed to Ashburton, Chagford, Plympton or Tavistock, the moor's 'stannary' towns – named from *stannum*, Latin for tin – where the manufactured tin was taxed.

In medieval times the tin miners of Dartmoor were a national asset, and were given exemption from ordinary laws, a fact which doubtless attracted some men to what was a hard, lonely and sometimes dangerous profession. The miners were subject only to stannary law (enacted by a Parliament sitting at Crockern Tor) which was administered by the Stannary Courts at the four stannary towns. Transgressors against stannary law were imprisoned in the Stannary Gaol at Lydford.

Today the mines are all silent, as are the quarries that extracted granite for prestigious building works. Now only the china clay works of Lee Moor extract wealth from Dartmoor's minerals. The moor is still farmed, but apart from the moorland fringe the farming is hard work for minimal reward. Increasingly, it is recreation that is the life blood of Dartmoor.

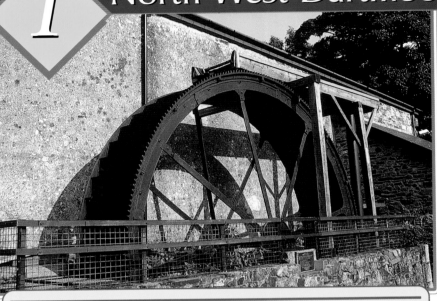

• OKEHAMPTON •

Lying just outside the National Park, but in the shadow of Dartmoor's highest ground, Okehampton is the main visitor centre for exploring the northern moor.

It is not clear whether the Celts had a settlement here – though there is an Iron Age hill fort to the east, above the East Okement: a Roman fort has also been discovered to the north-east – though they certainly named the river whose twin branches run through the town, calling it the Okement, the noisy river. The Saxons definitely had a settlement here, naming it after the river: their Ocmundtun became today's Okehampton. Okehampton now wraps itself around both the East and West Okement streams, the 'meet' of the two being at the northern edge of the town.

Once the scene of annual bottlenecks as traffic stuttered through on the way to Cornwall, the town is now bypassed by the new A30 and has regained the quieter bustle it must have had as the local market town in bygone years. To explore Okehampton start at the Museum of Dartmoor Life (there is a small car park beside it, and other car parks further from the town centre). On the car park side of the museum there is a fine restored waterwheel.

Museum of Dartmoor Life

White Hart Courtyard, Okehampton

The museum is housed on three floors of a nineteenth-century mill and houses a collection which explores the life of Dartmoor folk over the centuries. There are audio/visual and some interactive exhibits and a gallery for temporary exhibitions.

Gift/book shop, ☎ (01837) 52295. Open: 10am-5pm, Monday to Saturday, Easter to October; also open on Sundays (same times) from June to September; 10am-4pm, Saturday and Sunday, November to Easter.

The museum stands in a charming courtyard which also includes the Tourist Information Centre (once a small printing works), the Proper Job craft centre (with a range of locally made crafts) and the Victorian Pantry Tea Rooms, a good spot to end an exploratory walk. The craft shop and tea rooms are housed in old cottages. Leave the courtyard into West Street. A left turn here – crossing West Bridge over the West Okement River – then a right turn along Church Street and a walk along the cobbled Choirboys Path leads to Christ Church. It is a fine medieval church, though largely rebuilt in the nineteenth century.

Inside the church there is a monument to Benjamin Gayer (see Cranmere Pool feature box on page 16).

Almost opposite the exit from the courtyard is Market Street. On the corner is the Town Hall, granite built in 1685 as the private house of a wealthy town merchant. Further along Market Street are the Charter Hall and Market Hall.

Okehampton Charter Hall

The Hall was opened in 1973, the 350th anniversary of the granting of the town's charter. The Hall houses flea markets on Thursdays, Fridays and Saturdays, and a monthly craft fair.

☎ (01837) 53179 for details.

There are also Saturday markets in the Market Hall.

Turn right from the courtyard to go along Fore Street, soon reaching St James' Chapel, the town's most prominent building: the tower dates from the fourteenth century. The chapel was used by the townsfolk when flooding of the West Okement River prevented them from reaching the parish church: before the building of West Bridge, the river had to be forded.

To the south of the town – follow George Street from the junction of

Market Street, Fore Street and West Street – a road fork offers two further interesting visitor sites, though each is much easier to reach by car, being quite a step for the walker. The aptly named Station Road leads to the Okehampton Railway Station Visitor Centre.

The station was opened in 1871 by the London and South Western Railway Company which became Southern Railways in 1923. The line did not survive the Beeching cuts, finally closing in 1972. After lying neglected for twenty years restoration work began in 1994, though it will not be fully completed for several years yet. The old goods shed has been converted into a Youth Hostel. Trains now link the station to Exeter (summer Sunday service only), with buses meeting the trains to transfer passengers to local villages.

The trains of the Dartmoor Pony also operate, taking visitors the short distance to Meldon station close to the famous viaduct. Visitors can walk over the viaduct, which now forms part of a cycle route. This magnificent iron viaduct was erected in 1874. It is 540ft (165m) long and up to 150ft (46m) high, and is a listed building.

The other fork leads to Oke-hampton Castle, the largest and one of the oldest, in Devon. The first castle on the site was built soon after the Conquest by Baldwin de Brionne the new Sheriff of Devon. This first castle was 'motte and bailey', a steep mound being con-structed in this case, unusually, with material from a ditch around the motte base, below which was a courtyard (bailey) surrounded by a wooden stockade. The motte would have been surmounted by a wooden keep. In time, the wooden structures would have been replaced with stone: the motte is now topped by the ruins of a late eleventh-century stone keep.

Later, the castle passed to the Courtenay family who became the Earls of Devon. The Courtenays added to the castle, creating a strong defensive position, but then, as the

Okehampton Railway Station and Meldon Viaduct Visitor Centres

Partially restored station. Buffet, museum, model railway and model shop. Open: 10am-5.30pm Tuesday to Sunday and Bank Holiday Mondays, June to September. 10am-5pm Wednesday to Sunday, November to May.

The station at the Meldon viaduct is the highest in southern England, at 850ft (259m). The Visitor Centre is housed in the old quarry's pumphouse. Please note that access to the Visitor Centre is by train, cycle or on foot only. Open: 11am-5.30pm Tuesday to Sunday, mid-July to September. 11am-5.30pm Saturday and Sunday, October.

☎ (01837) 55330 Okehampton Station.
☎ (01837) 55637 Dartmoor Railway enquiries.
☎ (01837) 55667 Dartmoor Railway information.

Above: Ponies at Cherrybrook Bridge
Below: The summit of Yes Tor

• CRANMERE POOL •

S ome say that the name Cranmere is from crow pool, named for the ravens which frequent the area, others that this is crane pool, named for the herons which fished it in its prime. Today ravens are still seen, though the herons have long gone.

Although moormen had almost certainly visited Cranmere for centuries, the first recorded 'tourist' trip was made by John Andrews, a Devonian lawyer, who walked to the pool in 1789. In the next century trips to wilderness areas became the vogue among the leisured classes and the Pool became a popular destination, local folk acting as guides to visitors. In 1854 one of the guides, James Perrott, built a cairn at the pool. Inside it he placed a glass jar into which his clients could drop their visiting cards, and a visitors' book which they could sign.

At around the same time the peat wall which held back the pool was breached by unknown means (some experts wonder whether there ever was a real pool rather than shallow ponds among the peat hags, so that there never was a wall to breach). The pool drained away and Cranmere became the marshy area we now see. In periods of dry weather the pool all but disappears, but in very wet periods a shallow pool (or a series of small pools) is re-established. At such times the walker will also find the water forming pools in his boots as the ground becomes waterlogged.

When the vogue for guided tours ended, other walkers replaced Perrott's jar and book. Then, in 1937, the *Western Morning News* raised money to erect a stone box. This still stands at the pool, its door opening to reveal a rubber stamp for the use of 'letterboxers'. The name letterbox came from the early use of the Cranmere box: a walker would bring a self-addressed card to

The Cranmere Pool letterbox

the pool and exchange it for the one left by the last visitor, posting that on his return to 'civilisation'. The recipient would then marvel (or not) at the time taken for his card to reach him.

Soon other letterboxes were set up on the moor and the sport of letterboxing was born, walkers ticking off the boxes just as the Munro-baggers tick off peaks in Scotland. But Cranmere remains the number one site, the ease with which it can be reached from the north having done little to diminish its romantic appeal.

The Pool is associated with one of the best of Dartmoor legends, but one that is difficult to pin down because of its weaving of reality and myth. Benjamin (Benji) Gayer, one-time Mayor of Okehampton, is said to haunt the Pool, his spirit originally condemned to empty it with a sieve. When the clever Benji lined his sieve with a sheepskin and looked as though he might complete his task, the punishment was changed to weaving the sand at the bottom of the pool into a rope.

But why exactly was Benji condemned? There are two versions of the tale, each said to be the truth about the real Benji. In one he is said to have embezzled money raised locally for the release of sailors who had been captured by Turkish pirates – but local sailors from landlocked Dartmoor? In the other, perhaps more likely tale, Benji was hanged for sheep stealing, his body left to rot on a gibbet on the summit of nearby Hangingstone Hill (itself named for the execution). The howling occasionally heard near the Pool is said to be Benji's frustrated spirit rather than the wind.

need for a fortress passed, they made it more of a country house by adding domestic buildings. Eventually the site was abandoned, probably around the time of Henry VIII. It was used as a convenient quarry by the locals, the elements and time adding their own destructive forces. Today the ruins are in the hands of English Heritage.

The castle's position, on a spur of land above the West Okement River, adds a romantic touch to the gaunt, jagged remains. In spring the surrounding woodland is carpeted with bluebells, enhancing the beauty of what was originally the deer park of the Devon Earls.

Okehampton Castle

Romantic ruins of the largest medieval castle in Devon. Picnic site and woodland trails. Programme of events on summer weekends.

☎ (01837) 52844.

Open: 10am-6pm daily, April to September. 10am-5pm daily, October.

Okehampton is not only a centre for walkers on northern Dartmoor, but is the start (or end) point of two long-distance trails and lies on a third. The Two Castles Trail links the town with Launceston, while the West Devon Way reaches the sea at Plymouth on a route through Tavistock. The third route is the Tarka Trail (see below) at Sticklepath.

The Ghost of Okehampton Castle

It is said that each night the ghost of Lady Howard of Fitzford, near Tavistock, visits the castle to pick a single blade of grass. The story confuses Lady Mary Howard with Lady Frances Howard who reputedly murdered four husbands and was imprisoned in the Tower of London, but so good is the story that facts are not allowed to get in its way. Lady Howard is said to change into a black dog that runs beside a coach built of the bones of her dead husbands, driven by a headless coachman and pulled by headless horses. The coach and dog follow the old road from Tavistock to the castle, the dog biting off one blade of grass before the coach sets off on the return journey to Fitzford. Given the extraordinary nature of the haunting it is hard to believe the group is not reported more often – it could hardly be mistaken for anything else.

Okehampton from its Castle

Highest Dartmoor

Walkers aiming for highest Dartmoor often pass through Okehampton, taking the road south to the military camp and then the rough military road that heads south – with the occasional ford – on a circular route which passes close to the highest peaks and to Cranmere Pool, the moor's most famous feature.

To reach the Pool, the shortest walk is from the observation point (a pill box – OP15) at 602878. Here another road branches southwards. This too can be followed, though it is best to park near the observation post and walk. After about 900yd (800m) there is a fork in the road – if you reach a distinct left-hand bend you have gone too far. Bear right to reach a small pool (marked as Ockerton Court on OS maps, but known locally as Huggaton Pool) and turn south there, crossing uneven ground, peat hags and bogs to reach **Cranmere Pool**. It is not an easy walk and if visibility is poor it can be difficult to find the Pool and equally difficult to get back to the start. If you are not an experienced walker, chose a very good day or another objective.

Those walkers not wanting to visit Cranmere Pool or unwilling to risk the military road, can instead use the car park at **Meldon Reservoir.** There are eight reservoirs within the National Park. Six were built before the Park was designated in 1951. The Avon Dam was completed in 1957 and the Meldon scheme in 1968. Of these, Meldon was the most controversial as the site was chosen on the grounds of cost against another outside the Park. Many conservationists were appalled, seeing the reservoir's construction as against the principles of the creation of a National Park. The controversy may have been beneficial in the longer term, another proposal (in 1970) for a reservoir within the Park having been rejected. Whatever the merits or otherwise of the scheme, the reservoir is a pleasant stretch of water, some 60 acres (25 hectares) in extent and from the dam there is a fine view of the Meldon viaduct.

Walkers seeking a straightforward route to the high peaks should cross the dam, descend the steps at the far end and follow the path past Meldon Pool, once a quarry for the extraction of limestone. At first this was burnt to produce agricultural lime, but then used as ballast by British Rail. Beyond the pool is another quarry, this one for the extraction of aplite. This rare mineral is used in the manufacture of glass and the owners claimed the quarry would support the biggest glass factory in Britain. As with so many Dartmoor industries, the aplite quarry failed after a relatively short time. Now

follow the path to the Red-a-ven Brook and a Range noticeboard (see feature box on Dartmoor's Military Ranges, page 82).

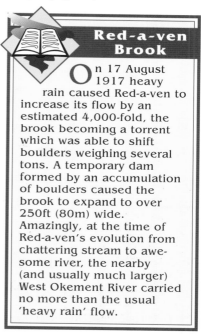

Red-a-ven Brook

On 17 August 1917 heavy rain caused Red-a-ven to increase its flow by an estimated 4,000-fold, the brook becoming a torrent which was able to shift boulders weighing several tons. A temporary dam formed by an accumulation of boulders caused the brook to expand to over 250ft (80m) wide. Amazingly, at the time of Red-a-ven's evolution from chattering stream to awesome river, the nearby (and usually much larger) West Okement River carried no more than the usual 'heavy rain' flow.

The brook can now be followed uphill: break right at any suitable point to reach the summit of **Yes Tor** from where it is a short step along a wide ridge to **High Willhays,** Dartmoor's highest point.

From High Willhays, the experienced walker can penetrate the real wilderness of northern Dartmoor, heading south towards **Fur Tor,** said to be the most remote place on the moor (ie. the one furthest from a road). The tor's name is from the dialect Var Tor, meaning Far Tor, another indication of its remoteness. New Agers claim Fur Tor is a mystical centre of Earth Magic and the haunt of fairies.

Less ambitious walkers can round the West Okement valley and return from October to March. Sadly the long transportation to Plymouth allowed most of the production to thaw and the 'ice factory', as it was called, soon stopped production.

In the West Okement Valley below Corn Ridge is Black Tor Copse, one of Dartmoor's three remaining upland oak copses (see Wistman's Wood in Chapter 4).

Fore Street and St James's Chapel, Okehampton

to the car park via Kitty Tor and Sourton Tors. **Sourton Tors** can also be reached by a shorter walk that follows a path which runs south west, parallel to Meldon Reservoir.

In the nineteenth century the Tors were the site of another moorland 'industry'. Shallow trenches were dug and filled by a nearby spring. In the winter, overnight, the water froze. The following morning the ice would be collected and transported by horse-drawn cart and train to Plymouth where fishermen used it to preserve their catches. At that time winters were much colder than now, ice being produced on many nights

Branscombe's Loaf & Cheese

Heading south-east from Sourton Tors the walker soon reaches Corn Ridge on which stand Branscombe's Loaf and Cheese. Walter Branscombe was a thirteenth-century Bishop of Exeter whose diocese included almost all of Devon and Cornwall. One day, while travelling from Okehampton to Tavistock, the bishop and his manservant became lost in a Dartmoor mist and finished here. Tired, nervous and hungry the pair stopped and the bishop is said to have called out that he would give anything for something to eat. At that moment a man appeared out of the mist and offered the pair bread and cheese. As the bishop was about to take it, his servant caught a glimpse of cloven hoof below the man's cloak – it was the Devil in disguise. The servant shouted a warning and the bishop dropped the bread and cheese which instantly turned to rocks.

• LYDFORD GORGE •

From Okehampton the A386, heading south, defines the boundary of the National Park. Just off the road on the left is Sourton, the pretty village that names the tors above it. On the other side of the road, a short distance south is Bridestowe where there are the remains of a motte and bailey castle within a prehistoric enclosure. The next turning right leads to Lydford, one of Dartmoor's most historically interesting villages and site of one of its scenic highlights.

Lydford Gorge, now owned by the National Trust

After the Saxons had succeeded in pushing the Celts westwards in the sixth and seventh centuries, **Lydford** was at the frontier between Saxon England and the Celts of Cornwall. The Saxons dug Offa's Dyke between their kingdom and Celtic Wales, but there was no such permanent boundary in Devon. This allowed the Vikings to sail their longships along the Tamar and to strike east towards Wessex. The raiders were beaten back, though King Alfred was forced to retreat to Somerset before finally putting the invaders to flight.

In the years of relative peace that followed Alfred built a series of *burhs*, fortresses, to defend Wessex against a renewed onslaught. On the western border of Wessex he placed four forts, at Exeter, Barnstaple and Totnes to protect the riverways into Devon, and at Lydford in case of a renewed attack along the Tamar.

At Lydford the Saxon fort occupied the sharp ridge of land between the River Lyd and one of its tributary streams. Within the ramparts the Saxons laid out a grid pattern of streets that the present village still follows. The importance of the Saxon village is reflected in its having a Royal mint, its coins – called Lydford pennies – being struck from locally mined silver. There are Lydford pennies in the British Museum, and also in the Royal Stockholm Museum: plunder from Viking raids or from Danegeld, the bribe paid by Wessex to keep the Danes from raiding the Saxon kingdom.

The Normans occupied the Saxon fortress site, but soon Lydford's strategic importance declined and the bigger towns of Okehampton and Tavistock became Dartmoor's major market centres. What is now called Lydford Castle, the imposing square block beside the church, was nothing of the sort, having been built as a prison in the late twelfth century when the village was the site of the Dartmoor Stannary Courts which dealt with those who had broken local mining laws. The prison was on two floors and a basement, its occupants being kept with little light or food, no heat or sanitation, and in constant fear of their lives.

Beside the Castle stands St Petrock's Church, named for a Celtic missionary active in Cornwall during the early sixth century. The present church dates from the thirteenth century, though it has been modified and enlarged since. In the churchyard is the Watchmaker's Tomb on which can be found an interesting inscription.

The Rune Stone near to Lydford Castle

Lydford Castle

The prison had a fearsome reputation often meting out punishment before guilt was truly established. The idea of punishment before judgement is based on the curious set up of the Stannary Court. A lower court tried and sentenced offenders, but its decision had to be ratified by an upper court. However, the latter had no power to overturn a conviction or sentence and as it met much less frequently was often in the position of ratifying a sentence that had already been carried out.

Below the village is Lydford Gorge, created when the raising of the Dartmoor plateau increased the drop of the river, adding to its erosive power. The corrosive effect of the river can also be seen at the Devil's Cauldron and Tunnel Falls. At both sites, but particularly the former, there are potholes rubbed round and smooth by swirling waters carrying boulders and pebbles.

The gorge is a haven for plant and wildlife. The river is home to brown trout, and dippers are often seen in its waters. On the banks pied and grey wagtails can usually be seen while the woods are home to nuthatches, great spotted woodpeckers, blackcaps and spotted flycatchers. The plant life varies from oaks in the gorge's drier sections to a superb collection of mosses and lichens in the damper areas. The Devil's Cauldron is particularly good for the latter, its walls hanging with dripping greenery. The gorge's flowers include the delicate wood sorrel, the green-flowered dog's mercury, wood anemone and, in spring, primroses, bluebells and violets.

Though well outside the National Park, it is worth visiting **Lew Trenchard**, to the west of Lydford, to pay respects to Sabine Baring-Gould to whom lovers of the moor owe a great debt. Baring-Gould was born in Exeter in 1834 and was ordained in

Lydford Gorge (NT)

Superb river gorge with lovely scenery reached by an adventurous walkway and a long waterfall. There are two entrances (fee charged), one at the village end, the other at the waterfall end.

☎ (01822) 820441/820320.

Open: 10am-5.30pm daily, April to September. 10am-4pm daily in October. Waterfall end entrance only, 10am-3pm, November to March.

The footbridge near to the White Lady Waterfall, Lydford Gorge

1864. He became vicar of Lew Trenchard in 1881 and spent the rest of his life there.

He was a gifted man, writing many hymns, most famously *Onward, Christian Soldiers*. His loving marriage to his wife Grace, a mill girl he met when he was a curate in Yorkshire (the pair had fifteen children) is said to have inspired George Bernard Shaw to write *Pygmalion* (the play which was turned into the musical *My Fair Lady*). Baring-Gould was a collector of folk tales and songs and it is largely due to his efforts that so much Dartmoor folk-lore exists. It was he who wrote down the words to *Widecombe Fair*: without him the song might have been lost. He is buried in the churchyard beside his wife. Lewtrenchard House, in which the couple lived, is now a hotel.

White Lady Waterfall

Legend has it that if someone falling over the cliff down which the waterfall drops sees the ghost of a white lady they will not drown in the river at the fall's base. But considering the drop – about 100ft (30m) – and the shallowness of the pool at the base it is unlikely that anyone would survive the fall long enough to drown. An alternative version of the tale claims that seeing the White Lady saves you from drowning if you fall into the river at this point, which seems more plausible.

• BELSTONE TO THROWLEIGH •

To the east of Okehampton is Belstone a pretty village grouped around two greens on one of which stands the old stocks. Nearby is St Mary's Church, originally built in the fifteenth century, but rebuilt in the 1880s. Zion Chapel, built in 1841, is now the Post Office.

From the west end of the village a track leads off: follow this to a track fork. Take the left branch for 50yd (50m), then bear left to reach the Nine Maidens Stone Circle. Despite the name there are 16 stones in the circle which is named for an often-heard tale that the maidens met here to dance on a Sunday and were turned to stone for their blasphemy. From the circle the walker can head south, climbing Belstone Tor to reach Irishman's Wall, which crosses the summit plateau of Belstone Common, extending into the valleys on either side. It is said to have been built by Irishmen in an attempt to enclose a section of Belstone Common.

From Belstone a narrow road leads to **Sticklepath** named for the path (locally stickle means steep) which approached the settlement from the west. The village is famous among geologists for the Sticklepath Fault which has displaced a section of the north-eastern moor. The bridge over the River Taw also achieved local notoriety when George III's coach became stuck between its retaining walls during a royal visit. To avoid further embarrassment the bridge was widened. Today the village is more generally famous for the Finch Foundry.

Finch Foundry (NT)

The foundry is an early nineteenth-century forge powered by three waterwheels. The foundry produced agricultural tools – scythes and sickles etc – as well as machinery for local tin mines. The foundry is still in working order and has regular demonstrations. ☎ (01837) 840046.

Open: 11am-5.30pm daily except Tuesday, Easter to October.

From Sticklepath minor roads lead to **South Zeal**, built in medieval times as a local market town. It is famous as the home of the Oxenham family – remembered in the name of the village inn – the deaths of whose members were foretold by a white dove fluttering above their heads. Most famously the bird hovered above Margaret Oxenham on the eve of her wedding. As she was in full health the omen was ignored: she was stabbed to death in the church by a jealous lover who then killed himself.

To the south-east of the town is Cosdon Hill on the eastern edge of which is a prehistoric stone row known as **The Cemetery** (or, sometimes, The Graveyard), though there

seems to be no clear reason for the name. The triple stone row runs almost due east-west, implying an alignment with the rising sun. The rows are about 150yd (140m) long and comprise dozens of stones not apparently chosen to be equal in shape or height. At the western end of the rows there is evidence of a small stone circle, and most certainly a *kistvaen* burial box. On the summit of Cosdon Hill there are Bronze Age burial cairns, while to the south, near Little Hound Tor, is another good stone circle. The White Moor Stone Circle comprises sixteen stones and has a diameter of about 66ft (20m).

South of South Zeal minor roads lead to **Throwleigh**, a secluded village with a restored granite church beside which is an early sixteenth-century church house. At nearby Higher Shilstone there is a fine sixteenth-century longhouse, the best on Dartmoor from that period.

Dartmoor Longhouses

Longhouses were, as the name implies, long buildings, relatively narrow and roofed with thatch over wooden beams. At one end, slightly raised, the family lived, the other lower end being occupied by their animals. The cooking fire stood on a stone plinth beneath a hole in the roof and a central drain – no more than a narrow channel cut in the floor – carried away animal waste. The arrangement must have been cold, draughty, smoky, smelly and would fail any hygiene standard you might care to apply.

The Tarka Trail

The ancient name for a river in Devon was Ta, explaining its use as a prefix in Taw, Tamar, Torridge and Teign. It was also chosen by Henry Williamson as the basis of Tarka in *Tarka the Otter*. Devon County Council has waymarked a long (180 miles / 290km) trail in Tarka's honour. The route is a figure-of-eight, one circle linking Bideford, Okehampton and Barnstaple, the other Barnstaple with Lynton, with a return along the South-West Coastal Path.

A fine section of the Trail, about 5 miles (8km) long, is called the Two Museums Walk as it links Okehampton's Museum of Dartmoor Life with the Finch Foundry in Sticklepath. The walk passes through Belstone village and then picturesque Belstone Cleave. Lovers of the book will know that it was in the Cleave that Tarka fought Swagdagger the stoat for a rabbit.

Above: The church at Throwleigh
Below: Belstone Cleave

• MORETONHAMPSTEAD •

This lovely little market town should be visited for its fine old buildings, as well as its position: the gateway to the western moor. Its main streets cross at the little island of buildings at its heart: one of these is the Tourist Information Office. It is possible that the Calculating Boy was born here as it is known his parent's house stood opposite the White Horse Inn, though it is more likely their house stood in Court Street.

The Tourist Office is a good place to start an exploration of the town. The White Hart Inn opposite dates from the early nineteenth century and was the scene of an infamous murder in 1836 when Jonathan May, a rich farmer, was set upon as he left. Beaten and robbed, May died in the inn. Several men were charged with the murder, one of them being sentenced to transportation to Australia. There must have been official doubts about his guilt – few escaped the gallows for such crimes in those days – and the man protested his innocence until he was eventually pardoned. But by then he had spent 41 years in Australia.

From the Office, turn left and walk along Cross Street. To the left is the Bell Inn, probably the oldest in the town as it certainly dates from before the Civil War. Further on, to the right, is Mearsdon Manor which has a twelfth-century doorway and other features from the fourteenth century. Ahead now is Cross Tree. The copper beech replaces a huge and venerable elm tree known as the Dancing Tree because platforms were often fixed to its branches. On these musicians would play and the locals would dance. Unfortunately the tree was blown down in a gale in 1903 and the new tree has yet to grow to dancing size.

Beyond the tree are the town's two floors high, arcaded almshouses, dated 1637. Expert opinion maintains that this date is for a renovation, the building dating from much earlier. In its original form the building was a single room heated by a central, chimney-less fire.

Now bear left to reach St Andrew's, a fine granite-built church dating from the mid-fifteenth century. Continue along Fore Street. Keystones, to the right, was once he town police station. It is said that two prisoners escaping from Dartmoor prison stole a car and crossed the moor to Moretonhampstead. Here they took a wrong turn and finished up in a traffic jam in Fore Street, right outside the station. A policeman inside recognised them from their descriptions and arrested them as they sat in stationary frustration.

Finally, as you return to The Square, as the island of buildings is known, look out for the Bowring Library to the left. This striking building is named for Thomas Bowring, a wealthy, Newfoundland born man who had local ancestors and donated the money to build the library.

Carnival week here, culminating in a procession on the fourth Thursday in August, is one of the best in Devon, and well worth attending. The town is also a good base for exploring the north-east corner of the National Park. But first, head south to visit Dartmoor's Miniature Pony Stud and Farm. Here there are not only the ponies of the name, but sheep, goats, pigs and pets.

Dartmoor's Miniature Pony Centre

Plenty of attractions for children including assault course and pony rides. Cafés and shops and the Field of Moor Dreams, a craft and garden centre.

☎ (01647) 432400.

Open: 10.30am-4.30pm daily, Easter to October (though later in summer and when the site is busy).

• MARDON DOWN AND THE TEIGN VALLEY •

Heading north-eastwards from Moretonhampstead a minor road climbs up on to Mardon Down, a last outlier of Dartmoor. As with the wilder moorland to the west, the Down is topped by a collection of ancient sites. The Giant's Grave is a large Bronze Age burial mound, and Headless Cross was probably never a cross but is a *menhir*, a prehistoric standing stone. From the southern edge of the Down – turn first right and look for the car park – there is a marvellous view of Moretonhampstead.

The North Teign River

To the north, Mardon Down falls away into the Teign valley, a magnificent wooded valley. Head first for **Drewsteignton**, a beautifully sited village on the moorland edge above the Teign. The village forms a square around its church. Holy Trinity dates, in part, from the sixteenth century but almost certainly stands on the site of a Saxon church. Julius Drew of Castle Drogo is buried in the churchyard beneath a granite memorial by Lutyens. To the west of the village are Spinsters' Rock and Stone Farm, while Castle Drogo lies a short distance to the south-west.

The Mythic Garden, Stone Farm

Stone Farm lies just south of the road which heads due west from Drewsteignton to Whiddon Down. The Mythic Garden is a 5-acre (2 hectare) landscaped arboretum and water garden (with important collections of native birch and alder) in which sculptors exhibit their work.

☎ (01647) 231311.

Open: 2-6pm daily, mid-May to late September.

Castle Drogo (its curious name derives from Drogo or Drew, the two apparently being interchangeable, a grandson of Richard, Duke of Normandy, the first Norman lord) lies just west of Drewsteignton to which Drew gave his name. The castle itself is much younger, built by Edwin Lutyens for Julius Drewe, a grocery millionaire who claimed an almost certainly spurious descent from the Norman lord. The castle

was begun in 1910, but the war and the shortages that followed it meant building did not finish until 1925. Sadly, Drewe only enjoyed his castle, and the marvellous view of Dartmoor from it, for a few years before dying in 1931, aged 75.

Castle Drogo (NT)

The National Trust has owned the castle since 1974 when it was given to them by the Drewe family. Inside, it is a mixture of the austere and the sumptuous. Some of the furnishings reflect Drewe's enthusiasm for his supposed ancestor, while others are the height of early twentieth-century fashion. The castle has an excellent restaurant. Outside, there are excellent gardens, planted with roses, herbs and rhododendron, and some good shrubberies.

☎ (01647) 433306.

Open: Castle, 10.30am-5.30pm daily except Friday (but open Good Friday) Easter to October.
Grounds, 10.30am-dusk daily, all year.

From Drewsteignton a steep road leads down to **Fingle Bridge** and the Anglers' Rest Inn. It is likely that there was a ford of the Teign at this point from earliest times, that making it the obvious place for a bridge, though there is no confirmed record of one before 1607. Despite that, the style of the bridge leads historians to date it to Elizabethan times. It was probably built for packhorses hauling charcoal from the local oak woods and flour from Fingle Mill

The entrance to Castle Drogo, now in the care of the National Trust

which was powered by the Teign. The mill lay about 985ft (300m) downstream of the bridge, on the right bank: little remains as it was destroyed by fire in 1894. With its pointed buttresses (whose tops were recessed so that packhorses could pass) three arches and wooded setting, the bridge is as picturesque a river crossing as exists on Dartmoor.

From the bridge the Hunter's Path climbs above the river, offering views across the wooded gorge. Two Iron Age hill forts defend the Teign near Fingle Bridge, Cranbrook Castle lying above the southern bank and the larger Prestonbury Castle lying on the northern, directly above the bridge.

Alternatively the path beside the river can be followed westwards. This is a beautiful walk, with sunlight flicking through the trees and the water just a stone's throw away. The trees are mainly oak and birch, but with some beech, ash and sycamore, and alder on the river bank. All three types of British woodpecker (green, greater and lesser spotted) and tree creepers can be found in the woods, while dippers, grey wagtails and kingfishers are often seen in or beside the river. There are otters in the Teign here, while the wood is home to fallow deer.

The Teign can also be followed eastwards, a path hugging the bank all the way to Clifford Bridge and then on to Steps Bridge. For the more adventurous, a fine walk links Steps Bridge to Mardon Down, returning to the river at Clifford Bridge and following it back to Steps. Further east, where the river turns south taking the National Park border towards Chudleigh, is **Dunsford**, an attractive village on the steep side of the valley.

To the south-east of Mardon Down lies **Blackingstone Rock**, a last remnant of wild moor. A car park here allows the view to be savoured. To the west are Hingston Rocks: legend has it that King Arthur and the

Devil stood on the these two hills and threw stones at each other, the stones forming the tors. Beyond the Rock the last slopes of Dartmoor are farmed and dotted with pretty villages.

Bridford lies in hilly country. The church, unusually dedicated to St Thomas-à-Becket, has an early sixteenth-century rood screen, a remarkable survival. Equally rare is the farmhouse of Bridford Barton which dates, in part, from the early fourteenth century. Close to Bridford is **Christow**, a village in an equally hilly position and with a fine seventeenth-century granite church. **Hennock** has a fine granite church and a medieval vicarage.

Between Christow and Hennock lies Canonteign, while a short distance to the west are the triple reservoirs of **Kennick, Tottiford** and **Trenchford**. Dartmoor's enthusiasm for collecting rain made it an obvious place to site reservoirs once the population centres of Devon had outgrown the ability of leats (dug channels) to supply them and increased awareness of public health had made leats an impractical source of water.

The first reservoir, constructed in the 1860s, was Tottiford, later extended by the creation of Kennick and Trenchford. The water is surrounded by extensive conifer plantations because it was once thought that such plantations 'attracted' rain. The plantations add little to the scenery of the high moor, but do make an attractive backdrop to the reservoirs, as well as offering a habitat to unusual species of birds. The reservoirs are popular with anglers. There are picnic sites and nature trails at Tottiford and Trenchford, but no public access at Kennick.

At 220ft (70m) Lady Exmouth Falls at **Canonteign** is the highest waterfall in England, but is not entirely natural. During the nineteenth century local miners diverted water away from the stream, which fed what is now called the Secret Garden Falls, into a leat which they contoured around the hillside to feed the mine. When mining ceased in about 1880 Viscountess Exmouth asked the miners to break through a rock formation so that the leat water spilled over a natural cliff, creating the new falls. At the base of the cliff the two falls combine to form Clampitt Falls.

Spinsters' Rock

Spinsters' Rock, a Neolithic tomb, has three upright slabs and a thick capping slab, and its name reflects the awe in which such sites were held by cultures remote in time from the Neolithic builders. The name dates from medieval times when the wool trade was a cottage industry. Three sisters who were spinsters – the name given to women who operated spinning wheels – are said to have erected the stones when they had a few minutes to spare while on their way to their buyer.

In medieval times it was often believed that such tombs covered buried treasure, digging for which often caused the rock slabs to fall. It is known that Spinsters' Rock has been reconstructed, though it is likely that the present form is a reasonable representation of the original.

Canonteign Falls and Lakeland

The falls are the centre-piece and there are two fine lakes, a restored Victorian fern garden, a wetland nature reserve, miniature ponies and other farm animals. A café, barbecue area and picnic site, a children's play barn and a gift shop complete the attractions.

☎ (01647) 252434.

Open: 10am-5.50pm (or dusk if earlier) daily, early March to mid-November; Sundays, New Years' Day and February school half-term week, mid-November to early March.

• CHAGFORD AND GIDLEIGH •

To the west of Moretonhampstead is Chagford, once one of Dartmoor's four stannary towns (where tin ingots manufactured at the moorland mines were taxed). The town's name – often pronounced Chaggyford by the locals – means 'gorse ford', gorse from the moorland which edges in on the town, ford from the River Teign which runs below it.

The Market House, Chagford

Chagford's relative isolation means that traffic has not spoiled its delightful centre, dominated by the 'pepperpot' market house, begun in 1862 and clearly modelled on the Abbot's Kitchen at Glastonbury. It is said that when the roof was refurbished in 1984 several hundred pigeon eggs were found beneath it.

In the porch of the delightful Three Crowns Inn Sidney Godolphin, the poet, then a young Cavalier officer, was one of three Royalists killed during a Civil War skirmish. Godolphin is buried in Okehampton, but his ghost is said to haunt the inn. The inn also has a bar named for Mary Whiddon, though her ghost is only seen at Whiddon Hall. On 11 October 1641 either during her wedding or just after it (accounts vary) Mary was shot dead by a rejected suitor. Elsewhere, ghostly chills are less in evidence and it is a pleasure to wander the town's alleys.

Chagford is also a good centre for exploring the north-eastern moor on which there are some fine ancient sites. From the town, minor roads head west reaching Batworthy, Scorhill and Gidleigh. Close to the road end at **Batworthy** – there is a car park just before the road end and space for a small number of cars at the end – is **Round Pound**, the road making a detour around it.

Round Pound

It is likely that the massively-walled pound dates from the late Bronze Age. It consists of a central hut surrounded by a walled enclosure divided into five 'paddocks', several with exits on to the moor, though it is not clear whether this is the work of a later occupant. It is likely that the pound was used by medieval shepherds and perhaps even by tinners so the paddocks and their entrance-ways could be much younger than the main structure. The true purpose of the pound is still debated, though most experts believe such buildings were for domestic animals.

To the south of the pound is **Kes Tor** on which there is a superb rock basin. Such basins were once though to have been carved by prehistoric man, perhaps to capture blood during some sacrificial ritual, but are now known to be the result of natural weathering. Looking north from Kes Tor, the visitor will see curious ridges running north-east/south-west and occasional circles of stones. These are the remains of a fairly extensive Bronze Age settlement, the stone circles being the bases of a series of huts, the shallow ridges being 'reaves', low stone walls which defined the edges of fields.

To the west of the Tor is Shovel Down on which there is a whole collection of prehistoric remains, perhaps second only to Merrivale in importance. There are five stone rows here, a stone circle and several single standing stones. As some of the stones cannot be seen from others, it is thought that the site represents not one complex, but a series of unrelated (though clearly not completely unrelated: they are, after all, on the some piece of moorland) sites. The southernmost row is the most impressive, ending at a large standing stone called the Longstone.

South again is a single stone called the Three Boys, its curious title arising from the fact that once there were indeed three stones, but two were plundered to act as gateposts.

Take the minor road for Gidleigh, but ignore the turn to the village, continuing to the road end car park. Now take the short walk to the **Scorhill Stone Circle**, one of the finest of all Dartmoor's circles and thought to be the only one which has not been reconstructed. Folk lore claims that the exact number of stones cannot be counted as the fairy folk move them as you are attempting the count. The circle is almost 80ft (25m) in diameter and comprises about twenty five stones.

From the circle walk south, crossing the Wallabrook clapper bridge

Above: The Scorhill stone circle, one of the finest on Dartmoor

Right: The rock basin on Kes Tor

to reach the North Teign River and the **Teign-a-ver clapper**. It is thought that local tin miners built both the clappers to gain access to Scorhill Down from the Teigncombe side of the river. Teign-a-ver was rebuilt in 1826 when a flood destroyed an earlier version.

Close to Teign-a-ver, a short distance downstream, is the **Tolmen**, a curious holed stone reminiscent of the famous Men-an-Tol on Cornwall's Penwith Moor. The hole is natural, formed in the same way as the rock basin on Kes Tor, but its strangeness caused it to be incorporated into local legends. It is occasionally referred to as the Christianity Stone and is said to ease the symptoms of rheumatism sufferers who crawl through the hole. From Teign-a-ver the wall on the left can be followed to reach the road end by Round Pound.

Gidleigh is a picturesque hamlet, but one that visitors occasionally miss as it is not the easiest place on the moor to find. The granite church is fifteenth century, a little younger than the castle ruins close to it. The castle was built by Sir William Prous, reputedly as a response to the more splendid castle at Okehampton. North-west of the hamlet an unfenced section of the minor road to Higher Shilstone allows access to the eastern flank of Buttern Hill where there is one of Dartmoor's most extensive collections of ancient hut circles.

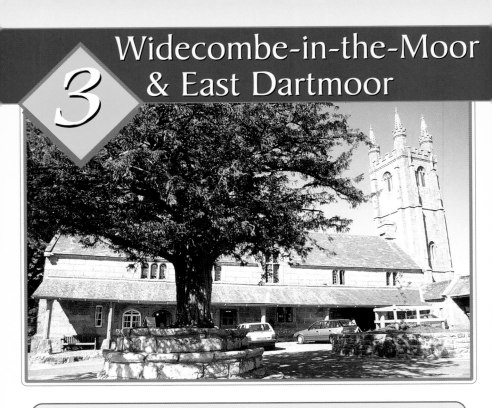

• WIDECOMBE-IN-THE-MOOR •

There is more to the village than Uncle Tom Cobley and all, though you could be forgiven for not thinking so as you gaze at the plethora of potential souvenirs. The church is late-fourteenth century and has one of the finest towers in Devon, paid for by local tin miners and a tribute to the wealth generated by Dartmoor's metal ore. The tower is 135ft (41m) high: its grandeur has caused Widecombe church to be referred to as the 'Cathedral of the Moor'.

Beside the church is Church House with next door the old Sexton's Cottage. Nearby is the village green, known as Butt Park. Park is the local name for a field, butt being the stand for an archer: in medieval times this is where the village menfolk practised archery, as required by the law. To the west is the Old Inn which dates from the fourteenth century.

The song which has made Widecombe famous refers to Dartmoor's most famous fair, a medieval live-

The Church House, Widecombe-in-the-Moor (NT)

Church Houses, often called church ale-houses, were built as church halls and village meeting rooms. They would also be used as brew houses, the beer being sold, together with food, to the congregation who had often travelled from outlying farms. The profits from the sales helped towards the upkeep of the church. Widecombe's house, which dates to 1537, is one of few that remain and it is still the village hall.

☎ (01364) 621321.

Open: 10am-5pm daily, mid-February to Christmas.

stock market to which folk came from all over the moor. The men mentioned in the song were from outside Widecombe and travelling to it to do business. The song is traditional, but was only written down when the Rev Sabine Baring-Gould, vicar of Lew Trenchard, came to the moor. It soon became popular and helped to promote Widecombe as a tourist centre. Today the fair still flourishes: it is held on the second Sunday of September, but is now more gymkhana, livestock show and funfair than a real market.

A fine walk, but a long one and one which involves a lot of climbing, follows Church Lane out of Widecombe, and then goes up on to Hamel Down, heading north to Grimspound before returning to the village by way of an old track below Chinkwell and Bell Tors. The route on **Hamel Down** (part of the Two Moors Way) passes a number of crosses probably erected in medieval times as route markers, but later inscribed to mark the boundary of the Duke of Somerset's estate.

Grimspound is the best preserved Bronze Age settlement on Dartmoor, its relative remoteness and large site meaning it has survived the plundering such sites suffered better than most. Its retaining wall is about 9ft (2.5m) thick and is thought to have been around 6ft (2m) high when completed. The wall encloses an area of about 4 acres (1.6 hectares). Inside are the remains of twenty four huts. It is assumed that the pound was to used to prevent livestock from falling prey to the wolves and bears which inhabited Bronze Age Dartmoor. The pound's name is either Saxon, Grim being synonymous with the Norse god Odin, or from a local name for the Devil.

Jan Reynolds and the Devil

On Sunday 21 October 1638, during a service at the height of one of the most ferocious storms ever on the moor, a 'bolt of fire' hit the tower knocking off one of the pinnacles. The falling pinnacle went through the roof of the church. Four of the congregation were killed, though a contemporary record claims not by the pinnacle but by a fiery ball that passed through the church at the same time.

Some have claimed this was an example of the little understood phenomena of ball lightning. However, a local legend claims that the tragedy was the result of a deadly game played by Jan Reynolds, a local man. Jan is said to have borrowed money from the Devil in order to pay gambling debts. On that fateful Sunday the Devil was due to meet Jan in the inn at Poundsgate. The Devil arrived to find that Jan had gone to church at Widecombe.

The Devil rode his black horse to Widecombe marched into the church and hauled Jan out. As he was carried up into the air a trailing foot (or cloven hoof) detached the pinnacle. Jan was carrying his playing cards in his pocket and the ride through the sky caused four cards – the four aces – to fall to the ground. On the southern flank of Birch Tor, to the north-west of Hameldown Tor, there are four fields still known as the Four Aces. The story is myth of course, but at least one parishioner is said to have claimed after the accident that as the pinnacle fell he saw a cloaked stranger run through the church and that the lifting cloak revealed cloven hooves.

The deserted medieval village south-east of Hound Tor

• HAYTOR TO BECKY FALLS •

Heading east from Widecombe the visitor passes close to the Ruggle Stone to reach Haytor. The Ruggle Stone is one of Dartmoor's logan or logging rocks. Natural erosion occasionally causes a large boulder to be perched on another, or on bedrock, by a single point of contact directly under the centre of gravity of the boulder. In that case the slightest touch will cause the perched boulder to rock gently. Logans were claimed to tell the future to anyone with the ability to interpret the rock's motion after they had asked it a question and set it rocking.

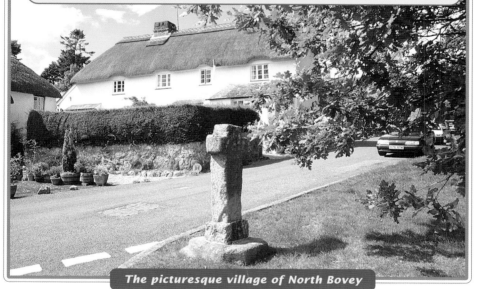

The picturesque village of North Bovey

Haytor is the most popular tor on the moor. It is easy to reach from the car park below it, but should be treated with caution: though it can be comfortably climbed on one side it has steep faces, which rock climbers enjoy but which it would be no fun to fall down. Be especially careful at Low Man, the second tor – set in rather than on the hillside – which is unforgivingly steep. From the tor there are great views – south to the coast and northwards to Hound Tor and Greator Rocks. From the tor a path descends rightwards to the old Haytor Quarries.

Hound Tor, seen from Haytor, is another popular spot with visitors. On the far side of it from the roadside car park, towards the rugged, but vegetated, Greator Rocks, are the remains of an abandoned medieval village. Excavations have revealed three longhouses and eight outbuildings, three of the latter having kilns which imply that harvested grain needed to be dried before long-term storage. Clearly Dartmoor's climate was wet when the village was occupied.

Quite when and why it was abandoned is not clear. Some experts claim that Hound Tor village was deserted when the farming became uneconomic, forcing the villagers to move into the valleys. Others claim that Black Death is likely to have killed all the inhabitants of such places.

To the north of Hound Tor is Hayne Down on which stands **Bowerman's Nose**, one of the moor's most distinctive tors. From the Down a short walk west visits the curious **Jay's Grave**.

North of Hayne Down is **North Bovey**, where the real John Bowerman may have lived. It is an extremely picturesque village with several seventeenth-century, thatched houses gathered around a green beside which is the fine church of St John the Baptist. The church has a fifteenth-century carved rood screen. Though much of the original paintwork and gilding has been lost and the screen was vandalised by the Puritans, it is still a marvellous feature.

Heading southwards, the next village is **Manaton**. The church here needed considerable restoration work after it was damaged in a storm in 1779, testament to the exposed village site. Outside the church stands the stump of an old cross: the locals are said to have carried coffins three times around the cross to disorientate the spirit of the dead – and so prevent it pestering the living. To the south-west of Manaton is Wingstone Farm where John Galsworthy lived for 18 years. It was at the farm that he wrote *The Forsyte Saga*.

Close to Manaton is the beauty spot of **Becky Falls**. The falls – often known as Becka rather than Becky – are a boulder 'tumble' rather than a conventional falls, created by the undercutting of a band of soft rock. Becky is a marvellous sight when rain has swollen Beckabrook and in summer, when the water flow is less, the moss-encrusted boulders, lit by sunlight flashing through the surrounding trees, are equally attractive.

Bowerman's Nose

This distinctive tor is said to have been created by witchcraft. John Bowerman was a hunter who one day came across a coven of witches and ran shouting through their midst, terrifying them. Days later he was caught by the witches who cast a spell which encased him in stone. When his family came looking for him he could see them, but they could not hear him, or recognise him in his granite overcoat. In time they gave up the search, but Bowerman stills looks out across the moor, trapped for eternity.

Interestingly, it seems that there really was a John Bowerman: he lived in the seventeenth century and was apparently buried in North Bovey churchyard. Could he have had a distinctive, angular profile which led folk to name the tor for him?

Becky Falls

Excellent water tumble and extensive woodland explored by marked paths. The woodland has many wildflowers in season and is home to tree creepers, nuthatches, pied and spotted flycatchers, goldcrests and woodcock. The site has a gift shop and café, ☎ (01647) 221259. Open: 10am-6pm (or dusk if earlier) daily, Easter to October and 10 days in late February.

Jay's Grave

Kitty Jay was the daughter of a tenant farmer who fell in love with the landowner's son. Seduced by tales of love and marriage, Kitty spent a long night of passion with the boy, only to be told the following morning that he would never marry such a low-born girl. Kitty went home and hanged herself in her father's barn. As was the custom, Kitty was not allowed a Christian burial, and was buried at a crossroads so her spirit, confused by the number of roads, would not wander.

Years later, wanting to know the truth of the tale a man excavated the grave and found it did indeed contain the skeleton of a young woman. The man created the grave with its simple headstone that still stands by the old crossroads. There the story would have ended, but it is said that flowers are regularly placed on the grave by a ghostly hand and that those who stay at the crossroads at night to try to watch are driven away by unseen terrors before the flowers arrive.

• LUSTLEIGH TO BOVEY TRACEY •

On the other side of the River Bovey from Manaton is Lustleigh. The Domesday Book notes Lustleigh's transfer to Ansgar, William the Conqueror's head cook, and that the village was the only one in Devon to have a bee-keeper. The village church is a neat building with a sturdy square tower. Inside there are several fine effigies and an inscribed gravestone, the stone dating from Roman times.

The village's May Day celebration is one of the most colourful in Devon. The May Queen leads a procession of maypole dancers around the village beneath a canopy of flowers held aloft by four canopy bearers. She is crowned with a crown of flowers on a granite boulder, in the Town Orchard, on which her name is then inscribed.

From the village a very fine walk heads south to reach the river, then turns upstream to follow it through the steep and deeply-wooded Lustleigh Cleave.

Heading south from Lustleigh leads the visitor to **Bovey Tracey**, named for its position on the River Bovey. In the nineteenth century the best ball clay in the world was mined locally and Bovey Tracey became famous for its potteries. Today the town, which lies just outside the National Park, is a pleasant, airy place worth visiting for its church and tourist attractions. The church is a fine granite building, extensively restored in Victorian times, but with several medieval survivals inside.

The fifteenth century Cleave Inn, Lustleigh

The House of Marbles/ Teign Valley Glass

Housed in an old pottery with distinctive firing kilns. Visitors can watch glass-blowing and the processes of making marbles, other games and toys, and glassware. The building has what is claimed to be the world's largest collection of marbles and two amazing marble runs, metal tracks along which marbles whizz, apparently in defiance of gravity. There is a café on site.

☎ (01626) 835358.

Open: 9am-5pm Monday to Friday, all year. Glassblowing can be viewed 9am-4.30pm Monday to Friday and 10am-3pm on Sundays, from Easter to September.

The tourist sites include the House of Marbles at the Teign Valley Glassworks, the Teapottery and the Riverside Mill, a showroom for the Devon Guild of Craftsmen. At Bovey Handloom Weavers, visitors can watch the weaving process as well as buying products made on site. A little further away – the other side of the A38 – **Orchard Paradise** with its collection of orchids will be on the must-see list of all gardeners, while **Gorse Blossom** will be of interest to visitors with children.

The Cardew Teapottery

As the name implies, only teapots are made here. The visitor can watch the process, or try their hand at the potter's wheel or decorating their own pot. There is, of course, a Madhatter's Tea Room.

☎ (01626) 832172.

Open: 9.30am-5.30pm daily all year except for Christmas week. Pottery tours are available Monday to Friday only and not on Bank Holidays.

Just west of the town, **Parke** is an early nineteenth-century house owned by the National Trust but occupied by the Dartmoor National Park Authority. The estate around the house is being carefully managed as a wildlife habitat. It is traversed by public footpaths and there is an annual programme of guided walks.

Orchard Paradise

Beside the A382 Newton Abbot road a short distance from Bovey Tracey. The award-winning Burnham Nurseries, run by the Rittershausen family, has a collection of rare and exotic orchids, including many which are endangered in their natural home. There is a picnic site and a range of orchid gifts.

☎ (01626) 352233.

Open: 10am-4pm daily all year (except winter Bank Holidays).

Gorse Blossom

Just off the A38 near Bickington, a short distance south-west of Bovey Tracey. The site has steam-hauled miniature trains, a woodland assault course and other, less challenging, play areas. There is also a model railway based on the Swiss St Moritz line. Fine woodland walks and good restaurant.

☎ (01626) 821361.

Open: 10.30am-5pm daily, Easter to October. Trains run 10.45am-4.40pm.

• BUCKLAND-IN-THE-MOOR •

On the south-eastern flank of the high Dartmoor plateau, just a short distance from Widecombe and Haytor, lie a couple of interesting little villages. Ilsington, closest to Haytor, and too often overlooked by those visiting Widecombe, is a fine place with a lovely church, a lychgate set on granite pillars and St Michael's Cottages, a delightful group including the old church house. But best of all is Buckland-in-the-Moor.

Buckland-in-the-Moor

Buckland-in-the-Moor is a lovely place, a collection of thatched cottages overlooking the woodland of Holne Chase. The early fourteenth-century church looks out across the River Webburn that joins the Dart close to the village. The church has a fine medieval rood screen with painted figures and panels, but is perhaps most notable for the modern clock face on which MY DEAR MOTHER replaces the expected figures. The face was a gift from William Whitley, lord of the manor in 1930.

Whitley was also responsible for having the Ten Commandments carved on two granite slabs on the summit of Buckland Beacon to the east of the village. The **Roundhouse Craft Centre**, on the road to Ashburton, shows local crafts and has a tearoom.

• PRINCETOWN •

Thomas Tyrwhitt, an Essex man, became a friend of the Prince of Wales when the two were at Oxford University. As a consequence, in 1786 Tyrwhitt was appointed as auditor for the Duchy of Cornwall and saw Dartmoor for the first time. He decided that what the moor needed was a town at its heart, its folk taming the wilderness to the Prince's (and his own) profit. He built the town, calling it Prince's Town after his patron (though its inhabitants rapidly shortened this to Princetown). But despite Tyrwhitt's enthusiasm Dartmoor would not be tamed and the future for his town looked bleak.

This was the time of the Napoleonic Wars and seeing the disquiet about the conditions of the French prisoners of war in the prison hulks at Plymouth, Tyrwhitt proposed the building of a prison at his new town. The prison was built by A G Rowe of Plymouth. It was built between 1806 and 1809 and cost £138,000, taking much longer than planned because of the weather and the difficulties of transport. It has been in use ever since.

Today, though visitors are discouraged from lingering anywhere near the prison, it is still a landmark which draws the curious. In Princetown postcards of it sell almost as well as those of other, more conventional, moorland beauty spots.

Presumably many arrive with a simple message 'Wish you were here' followed by '?' or '!' as appropriate.

The town's church is said to be the only one in England to have been built by prisoners, French and American POWs building it after the prison had been completed. The National Park's High Moorland Visitor Centre is housed in what was once the plush Duchy Hotel.

Prison Museum

At one time the prison had a working farm. In the old dairy there is now a small, but oddly compelling, museum to the history of the building and its more famous inmates.

☎ (01822) 890305.

Open: 9.30am-4pm Tuesday to Saturday, all year.

The forbidding Dartmoor Prison & North Hessary Tor TV Mast

• MERRIVALE AND VIXEN TOR •

To the west of Princetown, beside the B3357 are the Merrivale Megaliths, by general consent the finest on the moor. The complex consists of three stone rows, several cairn circles and kistvaens, standing stones and some hut circles. The northern, double stone, row is 200yd (180m) long and has a large standing stone – known as a blocking stone – at its eastern end. The southern row, also a double, is about 300yd (265m) long and is also closed at its eastern end by a blocking stone. The two rows are not parallel, and though they are approximately east-west, neither aligns with a significant sunrise or sunset. Almost exactly half-way along the southern row is a cairn circle (see below), a stone circle surrounding a cairn over a cremation site: its presence makes the Merrivale row unique. A short distance south-west of the cairn circle is an excellent kistvaen.

The T/A Stones

Not all the standing stones at Merrivale are thousands of years old. In 1696 Parliament passed on Act compelling the major towns at the moor's edge to erect waymark stones to help travellers crossing the moor keep to better known tracks in poor weather. Several of the local standing stones are inscribed 'T' on one side and 'A' on the other, the letters standing for Tavistock and Ashburton as the stones stood on the route between the two. When the first roads were built across the moor some of the old tracks were made redundant and many of the waymarkers were used as gateposts. The stones here are rare survivals.

The T/A stone near to the Merrivale stone rows

To the south of the rows there is another stone circle and several single standing stones, and heading south-east from close to the eastern end of the stone rows is a row of cairns laid out in a straight line. Close to the cairns are the remains of several hut circles.

To the south of the Merrivale megaliths the walker can use the trackbed of the old Plymouth to Dartmoor Railway (the P and DR) to explore the quarries of King's and Foggin Tors. The quarries and railway were other projects of Thomas Tyrwhitt, builder of Princetown. After his efforts with the prison Tyrwhitt was made Sir Thomas and appointed Black Rod, but his interest in Dartmoor, and specifically the area around Princetown, continued.

He decided that what was needed was a railway which would import lime to 'sweeten' the acidic moorland soil. His efforts to improve the moorland soil failed, but his quarries were successful at first, though he lost the contract to supply granite for London Bridge because the railway to move the stone took much longer than planned to complete. The railway was completed in 1827: later it was steam-hauled and became part of GWR, but it was never really profitable and finally closed in 1956.

Walkers who follow the old track will see some beautifully tooled lintels, part of a consignment for London Bridge, which were abandoned after the contract was lost.

High Dartmoor is a harsh place for animals, visitors being very lucky to see truly wild animals. What they will almost certainly see are Dartmoor ponies. So much a part of the moorland scene are these hardy ponies that when Dartmoor was made a National Park in 1951 a pony was chosen as the Park's symbol.

The history of the Dartmoor pony is a long one, hoof prints having been found within a Bronze Age settlement on Shaugh Moor, suggesting that 4,000 years ago the pony – or its ancestor – was already a working animal. From that time until the internal combustion engine became cheap enough to replace them, ponies were the beasts of burden on the moor. They carried the farmers around their land, hauled carts of farm produce to market, and, as pack animals, carried Dartmoor's mineral wealth off the moor. In the last years of the nineteenth century there was a sharp increase in the number of pit ponies required by the coal mines of south Wales and Somerset, and the Dartmoor ponies, small but very strong and hardy, were ideal for the purpose. But with the decline in moorland industries and the mechanisation of the mines, there was less need for the animals and numbers fell.

Over recent years there has been a dramatic reduction in numbers, from around 30,000 at the end of the 1939-45 War to about 3,000 today: not only are ponies no longer required as working animals, but there is less call for horse meat and no European Union subsidies for pony rearing. Most ponies are now sold as children's ponies, either directly or through riding schools. This has led to the ponies being crossed with more 'attractive' breeds. As a result, although some 'pure' stock remains, many of the moor's ponies are cross-bred and are less able to withstand the rigours of the Dartmoor winter.

The ponies are not truly wild: they all have owners, and carry distinctive ear or tail marks, or brands. But they are unbroken, coming into contact with their owners only at the pony 'drifts' (round-ups) each autumn, so it is advisable not to get too close as they may bite or kick. And please remember that it is against the law to feed them as it encourages them to stay close to the road: each year many ponies are killed or injured by traffic.

Opposite page: Protect the ponies by keeping to the speed limit

The Devil's Frying Pan

Opposite the Merrivale site is Great Mis Tor which, like Kes Tor, has an excellent rock basin. Mistorpan is also known as the Devil's Frying Pan because local lore maintained that after the Devil and his Wisht hounds had chased the souls of sinners across the moor and cornered them in nearby Wistman's Wood, the Devil would retire to Great Mis Tor and enjoy a fry-up breakfast.

Further along the B3357 towards Tavistock the visitor passes Merrivale Quarry, the last of Dartmoor's granite quarries to have closed. On again, the prominent rock pile to the left is Vixen Tor, one time home of the evil witch Vixana.

Wicked Vixana

The witch Vixana, who made her home on Vixen Tor, lived on the bodies of those sucked down by the bog below the tor, conjuring up thick mists to ensure they would lose the safe path. The last noise the lost traveller heard would be Vixana's gleeful cackle. But one day Vixana conjured a mist around a traveller who had a ring given him by a grateful moorland elf he had saved from another bog. The ring allowed him to see through the moor's mists and, if he twisted it, to become invisible. On the far side of the bog, still safely on the path, he heard Vixana's laugh and climbed on to the tor. Twisting the ring to become invisible he crept up on the witch and hurled her to her death at the tor's base.

Judge's Chair, on Crockern Tor

• TWO BRIDGES AND POSTBRIDGE •

Heading east from Princetown the visitor soon reaches Two Bridges. The bridges cross the Cowsic and West Dart rivers close to their confluence. The inn here is popular with walkers, the best of the walks heading north to reach Wistman's Wood. The wood is one of only three remnant sections of original moor oak woodland, preserved by the clitter among which they grow. This has successfully defended them from sheep which would otherwise have grazed away any new trees. The other woods are Piles Copse in the Erme valley and Black Tor Copse in the West Okement valley.

Postbridge has a good Tourist Information Centre as well as the old clapper bridge

Wistman's Wood is an evocative place, its oaks stunted and wind-distorted. On misty mornings the wood is one of the most romantic places on Dartmoor. But as well as being scenically attractive, it is of national importance for the mosses, lichens and liverworts that grow on, and beneath, the trees. From the Wood a fine walk now climbs **Longaford Tor** for a view of the north Dartmoor wilderness.

Walkers should now head south to **Crockern Tor**. The Stannary Courts dealt with offenders against the laws of the tin miners, those laws being enacted by a Stannary Parliament which met on an ad hoc basis. The

Parliament met here at Crockern Tor, chosen as it was at the geographical centre of the various mines. It is said that slabs were carved out of the granite of the tor for the representatives to sit on, but no evidence of this survives, and many experts doubt if it was ever the case. On the south-western side of the tor an almost certainly natural formation does look a little like a giant chair and is occasionally known as the Judge's Chair or Parliament Rock.

At Two Bridges there is a road junction. Bear left (the B3212), passing the old **Gunpowder Mills** to reach **Postbridge**, a hamlet which grew up in the eighteenth century as a stopping place on the turnpike road from Moretonhampstead to Tavistock. There is a small pottery shop at the left hand end of the cottages just north of the road near to the Powdermills. Look out for the little cannon on the left of the access road to the shop/cottages.

Postbridge is also the site of one of Dartmoor's most famous and picturesque clapper bridges. Clapper bridges are slabs of stone laid across streams. In its simplest form the clapper is a single slab laid bank-to-bank. Wider rivers required several slabs, pillars supporting the slab ends.

At Postbridge the granite slabs have been used to give a span of 43ft (13m) and the pillars are the tallest of any Dartmoor clapper, the East Dart River being prone to severe flooding. The pillars are also shaped on the upstream side so as to shed the applied force of a rush of water and, hopefully, avoid the collapse of the bridge. Many of Dartmoor's clappers have been torn down by flooding of the rivers they cross, but it is said that the Postbridge clapper was

only dismantled when the locals used the slabs to try to prevent a family of ducks swimming upstream (!) and so out of range of their cooking pots.

From Postbridge a marvellous walk follows the East Dart River up on to the high moor. Close to where the Lade Hill Brook joins the East Dart is the Beehive Hut, a poorly understood structure – is it a tinners' hut, used to store tools or something much older? Further up the Lade Hill Brook are the remains of several Bronze Age hut circles and the double stone circle of Grey Wethers.

The Grey Wethers Stone Circles

The two circles are each about 100ft (30m) in diameter and lie almost exactly on a north-south line. The circles were restored in about 1900, many fallen stones being raised, so the exact form of the originals, and even the number of stones, is a matter of some conjecture. The name reflects the fact that from a distance the stones look like grey sheep, the word 'wethers' being a West Country dialect word for sheep. A local legend maintains that a confidence trickster once successfully sold this 'flock' to a gullible newcomer.

Continuing the walk beside the East Dart brings the walker to a picturesque waterfall close to Sandy Hole Pass, one of the pleasantest places on the northern moor on sunny days.

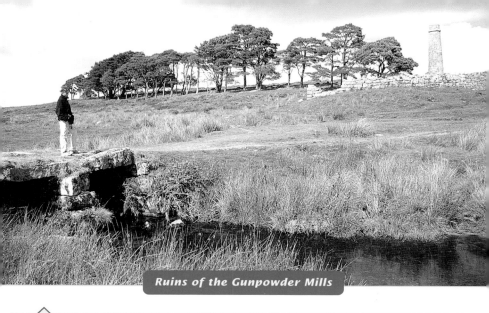

Ruins of the Gunpowder Mills

Clapper Bridges

No one is sure of the age of any of Dartmoor's clapper bridges. While it is almost certainly true that folk skilled enough to move and raise the stones of the moor's stone circles could have created simple bridges, there is no evidence that any of the clappers which now exist pre-date the medieval period when they were constructed as packhorse bridges. The Postbridge clapper is likely to be even younger, dating from the time of local tin mining.

• DARTMEET •

If, instead of bearing left, the visitor continues straight ahead (the B3357) at Two Bridges, marvellous country is crossed to reach Dartmeet, one of the most famous beauty spots on the moor. Here there are stepping stones across the West Dart River, the remains of a clapper which crossed the East Dart River and an old humpback bridge over the East Dart – the full range of river crossings. Although the crossing of the stepping stones requires care, it is worthwhile, the riverside path beyond being superb. Equally superb is the view from Combestone Tor, reached by a narrow road which leaves the B3357 just before Dartmeet.

• SIWARD'S CROSS & CHILDE'S TOMB •

A shorter journey from Princetown follows a narrow road towards Whiteworks, an old mining hamlet on the edge of the southern moor. From a lay-by car park on this road Siward's Cross is reached along a wide track. This fine cross dates from at least 1240 and is the most famous on the moor. It was broken in half in 1846 when it was pushed over by vandals, but repaired with a visible iron band.

The name is curious: is it from an eleventh-century Danish Earl of Northumbria given land in deepest Saxon England for supporting Edward the Confessor in his dispute with Earl Godwine? Siward is the

Siward's Cross

Old Siward of Shakespeare's *Macbeth*. However, there are others who claim the name is from a local thirteenth-century family. To add further confusion, the cross is also referred to as Nun's Cross on OS maps and in many reference books. But there were never nuns on Dartmoor so that cannot be the reason for the name: most likely this name predates both the cross and the Saxons, deriving from the Celtic *nant* which means a stream or stream gorge.

From the cross the track continues to the Eylesbarrow Mine ruins, while another track – called the Abbot's Way on OS maps, though it is not clear that there was ever really such a route – heads south-east.

From Whiteworks a difficult walk crosses Foxtor Mires to reach **Childe's Tomb**, which is associated with one of the moor's most tragic tales. The cairn is probably Bronze Age, but the cross that tops it is certainly medieval, perhaps even Saxon.

The story behind the cross involves a man out hunting alone on the moor one cold winter's day. He was a strong man but a storm blew up suddenly, the wind scything across the moor and snow falling thickly and the man became hopelessly lost and soon realised his life was in danger. Eventually, overcome by cold and fear, he killed his horse, slitting it open and crawling inside to gain warmth and protection from the wind. The warmth was, of course, short-lived. The man's clothes were soaked with the horse's blood and froze around him. By morning he was dead. One version of the tale claims the man was Amos (or Amys) Childe, but another version pushes the tale back many years and maintains the hunter was a Saxon called Ordulf and that he was a *cild*, the Saxon word for a leader.

The path to the tomb passes another cross (Goldsmith's Cross, named for a naval man who re-erected it), a very good example of a kistvaen and crosses the centre of **Foxtor Mires**. Many claim this bog was the inspiration for Grimpen Mire in Conan Doyle's *The Hound of the Baskervilles*, the story which pits Sherlock Holmes and Dr Watson against a huge black dog.

The Dangers of the Dartmoor Bogs

Foxtor Mires are among the very best examples on the moor of a valley or mire bog which forms where slow-moving rivers allow the valley bottoms to become waterlogged.

Although the waterlogged acidic soil is not attractive to many plants – though at the fringes lesser spearwort, bog pimpernel, bog asphodel and the insectivorous sundew can occasionally be seen – it has enough nutrients to allow sphagnum moss to grow in abundance. When conditions allow, the moss is bright green, making the bogs seem attractive oases in a desert of bleak moor. Do not be deceived, the entire surface is fluid, leading to other names for valley bogs – featherbeds or quakers. They can support the weight of a walker, but can also allow the same walker to sink knee or thigh deep and to be left floundering.

One famous Dartmoor tale has it that a man walking beside a valley bog noticed a top hat sat on the sphagnum. Gingerly he crossed to it and lifted it up. To his astonishment there was a head underneath, its owner asking for assistance in being freed from the bog. When the rescuer asked what he should attach a hauling rope to, the now-hatless man suggested would be best fastened to the horse he was sat on.

Stories of men being drowned in valley bogs are probably exaggerations, although some experts believe that ponies may well be engulfed occasionally, their long legs being very poorly designed for extricating them, particularly if they fall on their sides. But do not allow the fact that valley bogs are unlikely to kill you to make you complacent – being trapped in one could be a very nasty experience.

Goldsmith's Cross & Foxtor Mires

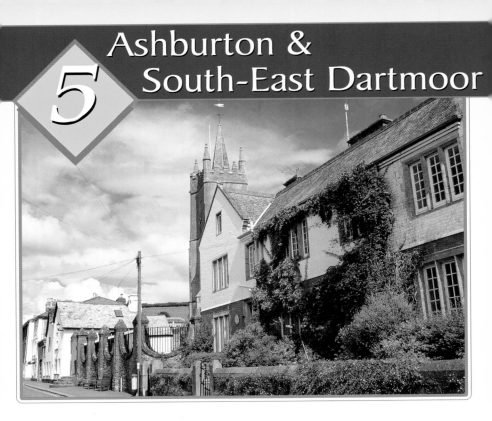

• ASHBURTON •

Ashburton was one of the four Dartmoor stannary towns – and the most important of them during the sixteenth century. It was also an important centre for the local wool trade. It is a charming place, now thankfully bypassed by the A38 dual carriageway. A walk around the town is worthwhile to see the slate-hung fronts of many buildings, a local speciality. From the Tourist Information Centre, bear around left to reach North Street. Turn right, noticing the House of Cards (now a supermarket), a seventeenth-century slate-hung gaming house. Further on, the hardware shop was formerly the Mermaid Inn where General Fairfax, the Roundhead commander, stayed during the Civil War. Ahead at the crossroads is the town museum.

Ashburton Museum

The museum, which occupies a former brush factory, has a good collection on local history and also houses the Endacott Collection of North American Indian items.

☎ (01364) 652648.

Open: 2.30-5pm Tuesday and Thursday to Saturday, May to September.

Turn left along East Street. On the left side as you follow this interesting street are a merchant's house hung with fish-scale slates and, further on, The Grey Goose, an inn dating from medieval times. Return along the street and turn left into St Lawrence Lane. The chapel, to the left, which names the street was given to the town in 1314 by the Bishop of Exeter and was the local grammar school for 600 years.

Continue along St Lawrence Lane, then turn right along a lane by the Silent Whistle Inn. This leads to a bridge over the River Ashburn. Look down here: the river is lined with granite slabs to ease the washing of wool. Continue along the walled path, passing St Andrew's, the twelfth-century town church, which

St Lawrence's Chapel

Fourteenth-century building with lovely tower. Inside there is a unique example of Devon plasterwork. The chapel houses the archives of the Grammar School and is the meeting place of the Courts Leet and Baron which elect the Portreeve.

☎ (01364) 652855/653414.

Open: 2.30-4pm Tuesday and Thursday to Saturday, May to September. In July and August the chapel is also open 10am-12noon on Monday and Tuesday. October to April by appointment only.

has a fine tower over 90ft (28m) high. During the Napoleonic wars many French prisoners of war stayed in the town – one is buried near the base of the church tower and the nearby willow is said to have grown from a cutting taken on St Helena.

To the west of Ashburton, across the River Dart is the **River Dart Country Park**, a private riverside park with a collection of activities. West again is **Holne**, a beautiful little village known to all walkers of the Two Moors Way as it is the end-point of the first day for those starting from Ivybridge. The church is fourteenth-century and has a superb carved pulpit. Charles Kingsley, author of *The Water Babies* and *Westward Ho!* was born in the Vicarage in 1819.

River Dart Country Park

Riverside park with a host of activities for children – tree houses, commando nets, rafts, slides (including the Demon Drop) and much more. There are fine walks through beautiful scenery and fly fishing on the river. The park has a picnic site, tea garden and a licensed restaurant (offering a carvery on Sunday).

☎ (01364) 652511.

Open: 10am-5pm daily, April to September.

The Ashburton Portreeve and Courts

Ashburton is one of only nine English towns (and the only one by Act of Parliament) which retain the Saxon office of Portreeve. The name derives from port gerefa – market official – and the appointed official (the first is thought to have been appointed in 820) was the local representative of the monarch. The Portreeve is appointed by the Court Leet, freeholders of the town, and holds the office for a year from November. The office is now symbolic, the Portreeve attending most local events and working to raise money for charity.

The Court Leet also appoints official ale tasters and bread weighers. The appointment of these officials dates from the time of Magna Carta when there were no official standards for bread and ale. The officials' job was to ensure that the townspeople were not being short-changed by unscrupulous merchants. There is still an ale tasting and bread weighing in July each year at which the Courts Leet and Baron wear medieval costume and walk through the town. The Court Baron consists of town tenants and appoints a range of curious officials – market and water course viewers, tree inspector, searcher and sealer of leather and pig drovers.

• BUCKFASTLEIGH •

Southfrom Ashburton lies Buckfast Abbey, one of the most visited sites in Devon, and Buckfastleigh, an interesting town with some good local attractions.

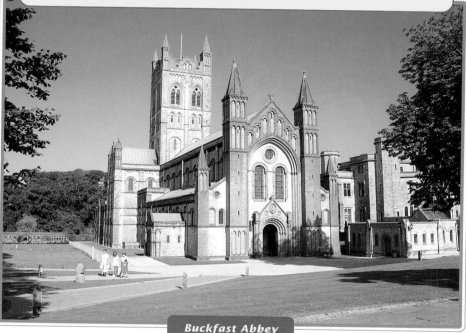

Buckfast Abbey

Buckfast Abbey was founded (or, perhaps, refounded) in 1018, by Aethelweard an Earl under King Cnut, for Benedictine monks. Buckfast does not seem to have been very successful, the number of monks falling and the abbey losing some of its land holdings within a few years. The decline continued after the Norman Conquest, but was reversed in spectacular style in 1147 when the abbey became a Cistercian house. The Cistercians encouraged sheep rearing on their Dartmoor estates and cereal farming on more fertile land. Dartmoor fleeces were not of the best quality but cereal production obviously fared better, requiring the building of the large grange barn near the medieval north gate.

After the Dissolution the abbey buildings decayed, but in 1882 the site was offered to the Catholic church. It was first settled by French Benedictine monks. A new abbey was built by a team of just four monks using manual rope hoists to raise the stone. The new church was consecrated in 1932.

Buckfast Abbey

Twentieth-century abbey on Saxon abbey site. The abbey church can be visited: inside it has elegant, soaring lines. Close by are two formal gardens, one of herbs, the other a 'pleasure' garden. The site also has a restaurant, a book shop and a gift shop which sells, among other things, the famous Buckfast honey and tonic wine. ☎ (01364) 642519. Open: church and grounds, 5.30am-7pm daily, all year. Visitor centres: 9am-5.30pm daily, April to September; 10am-4pm daily, October to March.

Buckfastleigh is a delightful Devonian town, virtually untouched by tourism despite nearby Buckfast Abbey. The town grew prosperous on woollen mills and leather tanning, the mills powered by the River Mardle, the tanning industry using bark from local oak trees. The town still possesses several of the pubs that kept the wool and leather workers entertained. Curiously, most of the pubs seem to be haunted, usually by female figures. The King's Arms has the strangest ghost, that of a young lady who, while waiting for her boyfriend, fell into an ancient well-shaft which suddenly opened up beneath her – falling down while being stood up perhaps.

Holy Trinity, the old village church, was built in the thirteenth century. Its hill top position – well away from the town – is explained by a local legend that all attempts to build closer to the town were frustrated by the Devil stealing the stones each night and depositing them on the hill, a curious story at odds with the usual form of the legend where a heavenly agency shifts the stones, favouring a holier site. The remoteness of the church meant that in the 1980s the building and churchyard became a focus for louts, and on 21 July 1992 an arson attack resulted in the church being almost completely destroyed: it is unlikely that it will be rebuilt. In the churchyard is the tomb of Squire Richard Cabell, alleged to have been a wicked squire in the seventeenth century.

The hill on which the church stands is composed of carboniferous limestone, Dartmoor's granite mass rising further to the west. The limestone is soluble, caves being formed

South Devon Railway

Collection of old steam engines and carriages (and a few diesels). Steam-hauled trips to the old GWR Littlehempston Station at Totnes, the line following the River Dart all the way. The journey can then be extended to Dartmouth by Red Cruiser boat. Regular special events. At Buckfastleigh there is the railway museum, children's playground, shop and café, ☎ (01364) 642338. Open: All year, but the service is daily only mid-May to mid-October. In other months there are trains only on specific days. Facilities are only open when trains run.

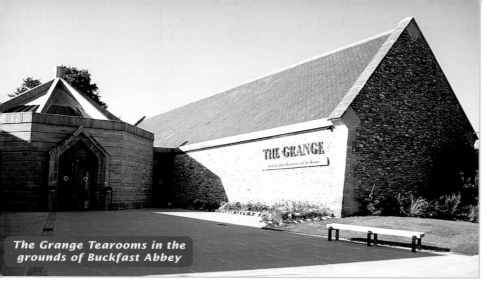

The Grange Tearooms in the grounds of Buckfast Abbey

by the rainwater percolating along fault lines in the rock. Quarrying on the northern side of the hill has broken into several caves from which the bones of prehistoric animals have been excavated. Some of the caves are occasionally open to the public.

To the east of Buckfastleigh is the terminal station of the **South Devon Railway**, the Old Dart Valley Railway, closed in 1962 but restored by enthusiasts.

Close to the station is **Buckfast Butterflies and the Dartmoor Otter Sanctuary**. Here a tropical rain forest has been recreated within which a number of typical butterfly species breed. Almost as close is **Pennywell**, a farm park with numerous attractions.

Buckfast Butterflies and the Dartmoor Otter Sanctuary

Tropical gardens with birds and free-flying butterflies, together with such exotic extras as leaf-cutter ant colonies and terrapins. The otter sanctuary is a landscaped outdoor area where otters are bred and injured otters cared for. A special viewing tank allows the otters to be observed underwater.

☎ (01364) 642916. Open: Butterflies, 10am-5.50pm or dusk if earlier, daily, April to October. Otters: 10.30am-3pm daily, March; 10am-5.50pm or dusk if earlier, daily, April to October.

Pennywell

Farm park, where visitors can bottle feed lambs at the right time of year, milk cows and goats and collect fresh eggs, pets' corner, commando course, flying displays by buzzards and owls, pony and donkey rides, and other novelties.

☎ (01364) 642023. Open: 10am-5pm daily, Easter to October; 10am-5pm or dusk, Saturday and Sunday, November, January and February, but open daily in school half-terms.

• SOUTH BRENT AND IVYBRIDGE •

To the south of Buckfastleigh is South Brent. As at Lydford and nearby Harford, the church here is dedicated to St Petroc, the early Celtic saint. St Petroc's is an early Norman church, though much restored, sitting picturesquely above the River Avon. The road which heads northwards beside the river reaches a car park close to Hunter's Stone from where walkers can follow the Zeal Tramway to Petre's Cross and Huntingdon Warren, or the private road to the Avon Dam Reservoir.

The River Erme, the railway viaduct and pillars of its predecessor, near Ivybridge

Zeal Tramway was built in 1847 when an attempt was made to create a naphtha industry based on peat extraction from Red Lake Mire. After three years the venture failed, but a few years later the tramway was bought and restored by a company extracting china clay from Petre's Pits and Red Lake. A walk along the tramway takes the walker into a wild section of the southern moor. Close to the tramway as Red Lake is approached, is Petre's Cross, named for Sir William Petre, a late sixteenth-century landowner and marking the boundary of his estate.

Huntingdon Cross lies northeast of Petre's and is much better preserved. It, too, is a boundary marker of the Petre estate. From the cross a short detour north visits the ruins of a chapel built by the Martin brothers and others who wanted the miners, warreners and other remote moorland workers to have a place of worship. One of the brothers was the Rev W Keble Martin, the famous compiler/

illustrator of *The Concise British Flora*. The grid reference of the chapel is 666 666, an extraordinary coincidence.

The **Avon Dam Reservoir** was completed in 1954, after the creation of the National Park, with an understandable debate about the correctness of such an undertaking. The road to it – which walkers, but not car drivers, can follow – passes the Bronze Age settlement of Rider's Rings, one of Dartmoor's better features from that period.

Ivybridge Viaduct

The original, built by Isambard Kingdom Brunel in wood and brick in 1848, was replaced in 1898 by a fine eight-arched granite and brick structure. Brunel's pillars can still be seen behind the newer ones.

Southwards from South Brent is **Ivybridge**, a small town, just outside the National Park, famous among railway enthusiasts for its viaduct.

Close to the viaduct is the Stowford Paper Mill established in 1787. Ivybridge is the starting point for the Two Moors Way, the route officially beginning (or ending, of course) on the Harford Road beyond the Paper Mill. **Harford**, the destination of Harford Road, is a lovely little hamlet comprising little more than a couple of cottages and a beautiful church. Inside the church are a table tomb with a brass effigy in sixteenth-century armour and a painted memorial to John Prideaux, a local man who became Bishop of Worcester.

From Harford a road heads east to end at a gate on to open moor. From here the Two Moors Way can be followed south to Western Beacon. The beacon is the southernmost peak of Dartmoor and lies at the end of a long finger of high moorland, allowing wide views in three directions. The walker can also head north over Ugborough Moor into the wilderness of the southern moor, following the Red Lake Tramway, built in 1912 to carry equipment and workers to the china clay pits at Red Lake.

Heading west from Harford the visitor reaches Torr – which can also be reached by heading north from **Cornwood**, an attractive village at the south-eastern corner of the National Park. Now head north to reach a water treatment works at the edge of the southern moor. From the works a track heads on to the moor, soon following the River Erme. **Downing's House**, passed by the track, is a tinners' cache, and a much better documented one than the Beehive Hut near Postbridge. The House was also once known as Smugglers' Hole because of a persistent story that it was used to store contraband landed on the South Devon coast.

The track ends beyond the house, the walker crossing rough moor to reach the **Erme Stone Row**. The row can be followed – look out for **Erme Pound**, an assembly of prehistoric walls and hut circles, across the river – to where it crosses the river. From here the row climbs Green Hill, but the walker can also follow the river to **Erme Pits**, the debris piles and depressions of a medieval tin mine and **Erme Head**, the source of the river.

Tin is alloyed with copper to form bronze, a fact that has lead some experts to consider it likely that tin was mined on Dartmoor in prehistoric times, though there is actually scant evidence for this. By early medieval times tin was being alloyed with lead to produce pewter, the main material for domestic items such as drinking cups, bowls and spoons. It was at this time that Dartmoor tin extraction became the area's most important industry. When the use of pewter declined, Dartmoor mining declined, but restarted when tin was again required for alloying to produce solders and for the production of plate.

The tin is present in the Dartmoor granite as tin oxide (cassiterite). Where rivers cut down into a lode the cassiterite is carried away by the stream and it is likely that ore found this way was both the first used on the moor and also led to the discovery of the major lodes. The first method of extraction was by 'streaming'. Here streams would be diverted, if necessary, and dammed, the breaking of the dam causing a rush of water that tore away the surface material, exposing the lode bearing strata. Streaming was very destructive of the landscape, and despite the centuries since its last use scars from the process can still be seen in several places on the moor. Mining took over as the easiest way of obtaining cassiterite as soon as the problems of extracting water from deep shafts had been overcome.

In the early tin workings the extracted ore was smelted on site, the relatively crude moorland furnaces creating a fairly impure metal which was then carried by pack-horse to a stannary town where it was re-smelted to form pure metal. Later, furnace design was improved, with waterwheels driving

Erme Stone Row

The row is 2.1 miles (3.4km) long, the longest prehistoric stone row in Europe and, probably, in the world. It is even more intriguing for not being straight, for although it heads almost due north from the start, it swings right, left and right again as it crosses the undulating moor around the River Erme's Valley. It also crosses the river. The line of sight along the row is not continuous and it seems that the row was reasonably aligned when sections could be seen, but not too well when they could not. At the Green Hill end there is a burial cairn. There is also a cairn at the southern end, enclosed by a stone circle of about twenty five stones. The circle is occasionally called The Dancers, an old legend maintaining that a group of young people were turned to stone for the sin of dancing on a Sunday.

The stones of the row decrease in height from the circle as the row heads north, though the scope for this rapidly ends. What is also notable is that the row seems complete – though there are gaps on Green Hill – the tinners having left the stones alone when searching for material for their own buildings.

bellows to increase air supply and so raise temperatures. Blowing houses, as these new bellows-driven furnaces were called, are a feature of many of Dartmoor's mine ruins.

Often, close to the ruins, mouldstones could be found. These were large granite stones into which square holes had been chiselled. Molten metal was poured into the mouldstones to form metal ingots. The building of blowing houses on the moor reduced costs as only the ingots, rather than impure material had to be transported from the moor.

A further refinement was the crushing of the cassiterite which made the smelting more efficient. Again a waterwheel provided the power, gearing turning its circular motion into the up-and-down movement of stamps which crushed ore between themselves and a granite mortar stone. These stones, with their tell-tale circular stamp imprints, can also be found at mine sites.

Wheal Betsy Mine north-west of Mary Tavy

From Erme Pits walkers can return over Langcombe Hill and Stall Moor, reaching a stone row on Stall Down. As with the Erme row this one is aligned almost due north and is not perfectly straight. Also on Stall Down is **Hillson's House.**

Hillson's House

The stones of one of the cairns on Stall Down were used to build a small, now ruinous, hut called Hillson's House. Local legend maintains that a local man found a child abandoned on Stall Moor and that he and his wife raised it as their own, calling the boy Hillson from his origin. When he was old enough the boy returned to the moor, building the little hut on Stall Down and living there, supporting himself by building eight-day clocks, several of which are said to survive in the neighbourhood. It is an intriguing story and clearly based on some element of truth.

• TAVISTOCK •

Though lying just outside the National Park few visitors will miss an exploration of this charming market town, once one of Dartmoor's four stannary towns. Tavistock grew up around a Benedictine Abbey founded in the late tenth century by Ordulph, a brother of King Edgar. The abbey was sacked by Viking raiders, but rebuilt and was one of the richest on the South-West Peninsula, when it was dissolved by Henry VIII.

Little remains of the abbey, but what does exist is worth seeing. At the southern (river) side of Bedford Square, where the Tourist Information Centre is situated, Court Gate was the main entrance to the abbey. Close to the church there is an L-shaped section of wall of the original abbey church, while to the south of this, across Plymouth Road – beside the Bedford Hotel – is Betsy Grimbal's Tower, a part of the abbot's lodging. The name is a curiosity. Local legend has it that Betsy was a nun who was murdered by her lover, one of the abbey's monks but the reality seems to be that the name is a corruption of Blessed Grimbald, a ninth-century saint.

The church, dedicated, unusually, to St Eustachius – Tavistock's church is one of only three in England dedicated to this Roman centurion martyred for his faith – dates from the early fourteenth century. It has a stained glass window designed by William Morris and houses the supposed remains of Ordulph, founder of the abbey.

Opposite the church is Bedford Square, which many claim to be one the finest examples of Victorian building in Britain. Beyond the glorious façade is the Pannier Market. The market is first recorded in 1105 and is still held here, weekly on Friday, though the present market building only dates from the mid-nineteenth century. The sides of the market square are now occupied by cafés and small shops making it an excellent place for a quiet coffee or some souvenir hunting.

Tavistock also boasts weekly antique/craft (Tuesdays) and Victorian (Wednesday) markets. At the Victorian market all the traders dress in period costume. The costumes are also useful at Christmas when the town has a Dickensian evening. The shops stay open very late and the hot chestnut sellers do a roaring trade.

To the north of the town centre is the viaduct built in 1889 by the South-Western Railway Company. The trains have long gone and the viaduct forms part of a walk which follows the old track. To reach the viaduct, which offers a splendid view of the town, head north from Bedford Square (passing the town museum), then turn right for the old station. Another fine walk follows the canal, dug in the early years of the nineteenth century by John Taylor (an engineering genius who was only 26 when he was engaged to build the canal) to link the town to the Tamar port of Morwellham 5 miles (about 8km) away. The Wharf, where the barges loaded and unloaded, is now the site of the

town theatre and arts centre. Nearby is the Meadowlands Complex with its swimming pool, sports facilities and picnic site.

Tavistock Museum

The museum is housed in the Town Council Offices in Drake Road and has a small, but interesting collection exploring life in Tavistock through the centuries. Every year there is an exhibition which focuses on a particular aspect of the town's history.

☎ (01822) 612546. Open: 2-4pm Wednesday, 10am-12noon and 2-4pm Friday and Saturday, Easter to October.

Finally, take a walk along Plymouth Road. At the far end is a statue of Sir Francis Drake, who was born close to the town (a short distance south-west at Crowndale Farm in a house that has long since disappeared) in about 1540. The statue was erected in 1883 by the Duke of Bedford (whose family, the Russells) were lords of the manor and grew wealthy on the local tin mining. It is the original, the identical statue on Plymouth Hoe being a copy.

Beyond the statue is Fitzford Gate, the sixteenth-century gatehouse of the mansion of the Fitzford family. The mansion has long since been demolished, but the family's name lives on not only in the gate but in the nearby row of miners' cottages beside the canal. The miners who lived here worked the copper mines at Morwellham.

Drake was born near Tavistock in about 1540 and became famous as a sea captain, and popular with Elizabeth I, for the riches he brought home from buccaneering adventures in the New World. He not only attacked the treasure galleons of the Spanish, but also wrested complete control of the slave trade from them. In 1577 he left Plymouth in the Golden Hind on a journey that was to take him around the world, the first Englishman to do this. He attacked many Spanish ships and cities on the journey returning in 1580 a national hero. He was knighted on board the Golden Hind in 1581.

In 1582 he moved to Buckland Abbey (which he had bought from the Grenvilles the previous year) and became Mayor of Plymouth. In 1587 Drake made his famous attack on Cadiz to forestall the preparation of an Armada fleet, an attack which has become known as the 'singeing of the King of Spain's beard'.

The following year legend has it that he finished his game of bowls on Plymouth Hoe before setting sail to rout a new Armada fleet. The game, and Drake's supposed comment – 'There's plenty of time to win this game and thrash the Spaniards too' – dates from many years after his death and is more likely to be myth-making than truth. Drake's harrying of the Armada caused it to seek shelter in Calais harbour where his use of fire ships destroyed its potential to land the thousands of soldiers it carried. The remaining fleet was then forced into the North Sea where foul weather finished what Drake had started.

In 1595 Drake and Sir John Hawkins took another fleet to the New World. This was much less successful: Hawkins died off Puerto Rico and the attack there failed. Drake attacked several other Spanish cities, but his intended capture of Panama failed. Drake died of fever in January 1596 and was buried at sea off Portobelo.

The Meavy Valley

• TO THE NORTH OF TAVISTOCK •

Leave Tavistock northwards along the A386. Soon a minor road leads off right to Peter Tavy, brother village of Mary Tavy, which straddles the main road a little further north. The village names are from their churches and positions. Each stands beside the River Tavy, with the church at Mary Tavy – the older of the two settlements – dedicated to St Mary the Virgin, while that at Peter Tavy is dedicated to St Peter. St Peter's is a fine, nineteenth-century building: the Methodist Chapel is slightly older. William Crossing, whose writings on Dartmoor still inspire many walkers and travellers, is buried in the churchyard of St Mary's.

Wheal Betsy Engine House built in the 1850s

From Peter Tavy a road runs up on to Dartmoor. From the road end a short walk reaches Tavy Cleave, the gorge of the infant river. The upper valleys of many famous Dartmoor rivers are shallow and wide, but the Tavy cuts a more dramatic path, its gorge steep-sided, the river littered with boulders brought down by floodwaters and having several picturesque waterfalls.

North of Mary Tavy the moorland view is interrupted by the old building and chimney of the **Wheal Betsy** mine. Wheal Betsy was once an important lead and silver mine its furnace fired with peat cut at Walkham Head. Despite Dartmoor being famous for its tin mines, copper, lead, zinc, silver and even small quantities of iron were also mined. Most surprisingly, arsenic was also extracted, chiefly for use as an insecticide against the boll weevil in America's cotton fields. Wheal Betsy is now in the care of the National Trust.

Across the main road from the ruins is Gibbet Hill. It is said that the name derives from cages set on the hillside in medieval times in which condemned prisoners were left to die of thirst and exposure, but that seems unlikely even for those times. It is more likely here, as elsewhere, hanged men were placed in the cages, their rotting bodies reckoned to be a deterrent to everyone who saw them.

From Mary Tavy a left turn leads to the pleasant village of **North Brentor**, with its neat church, dominated by **Brent Tor**, one of the moor's best known landmarks. A short distance west of the village, and just outside the National Park, are the **Rowden Gardens**.

Rowden Gardens

On the Liddaton/Chillaton road to the west of North Brentor. The gardens are famous for their ponds and aquatic plants, but also have fine collections of irises and ferns and National Collections of polygonium and celandine. In all there are over 3,000 species of plant to be seen. Plants for sale.

☎ (01822) 810275.

Open: 10am-5pm Saturday, Sunday and Bank Holidays, April to October; November to March by appointment only.

Brent Tor is topped by the famous landmark of St Michael's Church. Legend has it that the church was built by a rich merchant returning to Devon who, fearing his ship would be lost in a storm, vowed to build a church if he survived. Another legend claims that the Archangel Michael built the church, but only after a prolonged battle with the Devil: every night after Michael had worked on the church the Devil would remove the stones. Finally, the exasperated archangel hid to discover the source of his torment. Seeing the Devil he hurled a granite boulder at him, hitting him on the head. The Devil fled and Michael completed his work.

The church – which tops a cone of basaltic lava rather than a cone of Dartmoor granite – dates from the early twelfth century and seems to have been the work of Robert Giffard, a member of a powerful Norman family which owned land in Devon. It is a small church with a stout tower, the whole building embattled, and is a landmark for miles.

• BUCKLAND AND THE ABBEY •

Heading south from Tavistock the visitor goes through Horrabridge to reach Yelverton. From Horrabridge minor roads follow the Walkham Valley, reaching Walkhampton. Here, the church stands away from the rest of the village in one of the most dramatic settings on the moor. Close to the church is the Church House which has been converted into private dwellings. Within the main village the school is Victorian replacing one of 1719, a very early foundation. Further on is Sampford Spinney, a secluded hamlet crammed between Pew Tor and the Walkham Valley. The old manor house, now a farm, dates from the 1600s.

Buckland Abbey

Yelverton has an ancient name and one that is poorly understood – is it from elver, a young eel or from El's ford, perhaps after a Saxon settler: either has problems as there are neither eels nor fords locally. It is, however, a comparatively new place, growing around Tyrwhitt's railway (see Chapter 4) and the new west Dartmoor roads. Today, the track of the old railway is the Plym Valley Path/Cycle Track that can be followed from Clearbrook (just south of Yelverton) to Plymouth. To the right as the visitor enters Yelverton from Horrabridge is the **Yelverton Paperweight Centre**.

Yelverton Paperweight Centre

The Centre houses the Broughton Collection of paperweights which includes both antique and modern examples, many of them extremely beautiful. The Centre also has a permanent display of paintings by local artists. ☎ (01822) 854250. Open: 10am-5pm Monday to Saturday, two weeks before Easter to October plus Sundays from June to mid-September; 1-5pm Wednesday, 10am-5pm Saturday, November to two weeks before Easter (but open 10am-5pm Monday to Saturday 1st-24th December).

From Yelverton a short trip west, outside the National Park, visits two excellent sites. **Buckland Abbey** was founded in 1273 by Amicia, Countess of Devon, for Cistercian monks, a brotherhood who deliberately chose wild (but invariably beautiful) sites for their houses. The monks at Buckland would have enjoyed (or endured, depending upon your point of view) a hard life of physical toil and canonical prayer with little time for sleep and almost no comforts. However, their hard work on the land revolutionised British farming, particularly by the introduction of huge herds of sheep and the development of a more sophisticated wool industry. But as with all monasteries, Buckland was dissolved by Henry VIII, its land and buildings passing to Sir Richard Grenville.

Sir Richard's son – also Richard – was captain of the *Mary Rose* and drowned when it sank off Portsmouth in 1545. The Grenvilles converted the abbey buildings into a private house and it was here, from 1582 until 1592, that Sir Francis Drake lived.

There is a superb Georgian Staircase and an exhibition on the history of the abbey and its buildings; the Great Hall, built by Sir Richard Grenville, is one of the finest examples in Britain; and the kitchen and chapel are equally fascinating. Elsewhere, the Great Barn is a marvel: it dates from the thirteenth century and, at 159ft (48m) long and 60ft (18m) to the ridge top, is one of the largest in Britain. The oak-beamed roof is wonderful.

Buckland Abbey (NT)

Cistercian abbey restored as Elizabethan mansion, with excellent Drake memorabilia including the famous drum. Huge tithe barn and old sheds that are now craft workshops and restaurant, ☎ (01822) 853607. Open: 10.30am-5.30pm daily except Thursday, Easter to October; 2-5pm Saturday and Sunday, November, December and mid-February to Easter. The craft workshops are open all year, but individual times vary.

Not far from Buckland Abbey is the second excellent site, the Garden House, near the romantically-named village of **Buckland Monachorum**. The church here has several monuments to members of the Drake family. The **Garden House** is an old vicarage (of which only the ruin known as the Tower remains) bought in 1945 by Lionel and Katharine Fortescue. They have lovingly restored a walled garden and created the garden which surrounds it. Any attempt to describe the garden would fail: it is a masterpiece of colour and form, but special mention must be made of the acers, the wisteria bridge and the herbaceous glade.

The Garden House

Near Buckland Monachorum and Buckland Abbey. Magnificent 8-acre (3 hectare) garden including huge walled garden and expansive shrub, flower and tree areas.
☎ (01822) 854769. Open: 10.30am-5pm daily, March to October.

Staying within the National Park, a minor road from the huge Yelverton roundabout leads to Meavy. On the village green stand the old cross and a very old oak tree. It has been suggested that the tree is as old as the church, but that would make it at least 700 years old as the church has thirteenth-century origins. The old Church House is now the Royal Oak Inn. On the wall of the village school is a replica of Drake's Drum (made famous by the poem of Sir Henry Newbolt) once used to summon children to lessons.

To the north-east of the village is **Burrator Reservoir**. In 1898 the upper valley of the River Meavy was dammed to produce a reservoir to supply the growing needs of Plymouth/Devonport. Initially the reservoir had a capacity of about 650 million gallons (3,000 million litres) but was enlarged to about 1,000 million gallons (4,500 million litres) in 1928. The dam that holds back the water is faced with 6 ton granite blocks. Below the dam the now-dry channel of Drake's Leat can be seen.

Rising above the northern edge of the reservoir are the wooded slopes of Sharpitor. A path through the forest reaches open moor and, soon after, the stream running down from **Crazy Well Pool**. The pool is not natural, but a spring-filled mining hollow. Legend has it that it is bottomless, a legend supported by a story that the village folk of Walkhampton, to the west, in whose parish the pool lies, tied the church bell-ropes together and lowered them into the water to try to plumb the depth. They failed, confirming, in their own minds at least, the theory. In fact, the pool is about 15ft (5m) deep.

Drake's Leat

As early as the 1560s it was proposed to cut a leat from Dartmoor to Plymouth to supply drinking water to the town, but it was not until an Act of Parliament in 1585 that the city was finally authorised to 'digge a Trench throughe and over all the landes and groundes lying between Plymouth and anye parts of the said river of Mew'. The river was, of course, the Meavy.

Despite the Act, it was a further five years before Sir Francis Drake, when Mayor of Plymouth, finally got the project underway by digging the first turf. The 18 mile (29km) leat was begun in December 1590 and completed in April 1591, having been cut at the astonishing rate of 1 mile (1.6km) per week. It is often claimed that the leat was the greatest of all Tudor engineering feats. The leat supplied Plymouth for more than 300 years until it was replaced by one derived from the Burrator reservoir.

Granite comprises crystals of quartz, feldspar and mica. Coarse-grained rock, in which the crystals are large, has more and deeper fissures that allow rainwater to penetrate deep into the rock attacking the feldspar crystals The decomposed feldspar forms a powder which, in its purest form, is called kaolin after Kao Lin mountain in China where the fine clay was first worked. Kaolin – china clay – is used to create the finest porcelain.

It is claimed that the south-west's china clay industry started in the mid-eighteenth century when William Cookworthy, a Quaker from Kingsbridge, on the south Devon coast, realised the potential of the kaolin deposits when he was visiting Hensbarrow, near Bodmin. The Cornish tin industry was in decline so there was no shortage of workers when Cookworthy decided to dig the clay. He opened a factory in Plymouth and there, in 1768, he produced the first genuine English porcelain.

Not until 1830 was it realised that Dartmoor also had deposits of kaolin, though these lie only on the southern edge of the moor. Only the deposits on Lee Moor, to the east of Shaugh Prior were found to be commercially viable: by the mid-nineteenth century there were several mines on the moor. The kaolin is either dug out of the moor and transferred to settling tanks, or washed into tanks by water sprays. The settling allows clay particles to settle out. This 'mud' is then baked to produce pure kaolin. Once the clay was used almost exclusively in the making of porcelain, but today that is only a minor usage, over 80 per cent being used in the production of paper. Other uses include textiles and cosmetics.

Much more sinister is the story that each evening the pool speaks the name of the next person to die in Walkhampton parish. So fearful of hearing their own name were the locals that no one would approach the pool at dusk. It was also said that on Midsummer's Eve the face on the next person in the parish to die could be seen in the pool. As has often been noted, this is a strange story as anyone peering into the pool was likely to see their own reflection.

To the north of the pool, heading uphill, is Devonport Leat. If you turn left and follow the channel around Raddick Hill you will see one of the oddities of Dartmoor, the man-made leat scampering down a gentle wa-terfall to cross an aqueduct over the River Meavy. The original aqueduct was wooden, supported on the same granite piers that hold up the present channel.

Close to the reservoir's southern tip is **Sheepstor**, a picturesque hamlet, dark-stoned cottages huddled around a typical moorland church. The strange carving above the church's front porch dates from the seventeenth century (the church is a century older). The carving shows a skull, with bones in its mouth and ears of corn sprouting from its eye sockets, above an hourglass. The skull and hourglass reminded the congregation that death comes to everyone, but that new life sprang from death. In the churchyard are

Devonport Leat

Two centuries after the completion of Drake's Leat there was a need for an enhanced water supply. Devonport, the naval dockyard, and the town that grew up around, had developed a significant thirst, but Plymouth, which saw itself in competition with the new town, was reluctant to satisfy that thirst from its own supply. Samuel Johnson, visiting Plymouth in 1762, speaking of the inhabitants of Devonport, put it succinctly – 'Let them die of thirst, they shall not have a drop'. Hardly the most charitable of attitudes. It seems to have prevailed though, at least in part, as in 1793 a new leat was dug. This was a much longer channel taking water from the West Dart. From close to Burrator Reservoir's southern end the two leats (Drake's and what is now called Devonport Leat, though it was originally the Dock Leat) run very close together. From Dousland the Devonport Leat was piped, rather than channelled, to the town. Much of the work of digging the leat was carried out by French prisoners of the Napoleonic Wars.

the graves of three English-born Rajahs of Sarawak.

From Sheepstor a narrow road ventures into the wilderness of southern Dartmoor. From the road end, where limited parking is available, a track heads across the moor, passing a tree-shrouded Scout hut. Turning right from this track another reaches **Drizzlecombe** with its collection of prehistoric sites. The valley's name is a mistake, an early surveyor mishearing the local dialect rendering of Thrushel Combe, skylark valley. The sites include the tallest of Dartmoor's standing stones – 14ft (4.3m) – several other standing stones, stone rows, hut circles and pounds and the Giant's Basin, one of the biggest burial cairns on the moor.

To the south-west of the valley is Ditsworthy Warren, a vast rabbit warren. Such warrens are man-made (in their earliest form they are called pillow mounds) and supplied meat for the local miners. The warren was patrolled by a warrener who lived on site, netted the rabbits and controlled foxes and stoats.

Continuing along the track the walker soon reaches the ruins of the **Eylesbarrow Mine**. Eylesbarrow was one of the later moorland ventures and was also the last active Dartmoor tin mine. Here new mining techniques were used, sinking vertical shafts into the lode and tunnelling horizontally along it, with water being extracted by steam engine. In addition to the mine shafts there are the remains of a dressing floor where ore was washed to grade the rock so that gravel and other unwanted material could be extracted and dumped. After washing, the ore was crushed in a stamp mill and then smelted.

To the south of Meavy is **Shaugh Prior** a long, linear village close to the beautiful Plym Valley. The village has terraced cottages built for china clay workers during the early years of the industry. The medieval font cover in the church is said to have been discovered in a local cattle shed. From nearby Shaugh Bridge a fine walk follows an old china clay pipeline to Cadover Bridge, with views over the Lee

Moor china clay works, then returns past the Dewerstone. Dewer is said to be a local name for the Devil and in legend he and his hounds chased sinners across the moor causing them to throw themselves off the rock in terror. The Devil then collected their souls at the base.

The Rajahs of Sarawak

James Brooke was born in Bengal in 1803, the son of an East India Company judge. In 1839 he was asked by the Governor of Singapore to sail to Sarawak to present gifts and thanks to the Rajah for his kindness to a group of shipwrecked British sailors. When Brooke arrived he found the country in turmoil, pirates and rebels terrorising the population. He helped to restore peace and the grateful locals asked him to become the new Rajah. He accepted and remained Rajah until 1863, seeing Sarawak recognised as an independent country and being made a KCB by Queen Victoria for his efforts.

He retired to Sheepstor where he died in 1868. He is, rather surprisingly, buried beneath a tomb of Aberdeen, rather than Dartmoor, granite. Brooke never married, and was to have been succeeded as Rajah by his nephew, but he, too, died in 1868. A younger nephew (Charles Anthony Johnson, who took the surname Brooke) therefore succeeded. He, in turn, was succeeded by his son Charles Vyner de Windt Brooke as the 3rd Rajah. This last Brooke Rajah died in 1963.

One particularly gruesome tale relates that an old farmer met a man carrying a sack away from the base of the rock. In failing light and with failing eyesight the farmer did not recognise the Devil and, assuming the man was a hunter, asked whether he had had a successful day. The Devil laughed and thrust the bag at the former telling him he was welcome to the catch. The gleeful old man hurried home and called to his wife to come and see what he had got. When the pair emptied the sack it contained the broken body of their son.

From the rock there is a fine view across the Plym Valley. On clear days Plymouth Breakwater can be seen.

The old village cross and oak tree, Meavy

The Ministry of Defence has a large training area on the northern moor that includes three live firing ranges. Live firing takes place on only a few days each year and at all other times the public has access to the ranges in exactly the same way that access is granted to the moor's other public access areas.

The ranges are called Okehampton, Merrivale and Willsworthy. On the ground the ranges are indicated by Range Posts in red and white, and by Range Notice Boards on the main approaches which give range information. When the ranges are in use red flags are flown from flagpoles erected on certain high points. If the firing is at night these show red lights. When the flags or lights are showing, entry into the ranges is forbidden. **(It is also, of course, extremely dangerous.)** In addition to live firing, so-called dry training also takes place within the ranges. This involves pyrotechnics and blank ammunition which sound like live firing but are not. Access is permitted when such dry training is in progress.

When you are walking within the ranges do not pick up or disturb any metal objects. Such actions are potentially dangerous and are an offence under MoD Range Bylaws. Any object discovered should be reported to the police or the Camp Commandant of Okehampton Camp.

Please note that the ranges butt on to each other. If, therefore, there is firing on two or all ranges simultaneously there is no safe corridor between them.

Information on Firing Times can be obtained in advance, to avoid red flags spoiling your trip, by reading local newspapers on Fridays, or by checking the notice boards in local police stations. The National Park Information offices and some local post offices and pubs also display the times.

There is also a telephone answering service on the following numbers:

Exeter ☎ (01392) 270164

Okehampton ☎ (01837) 52939 (answering service)

Paignton ☎ (01803) 559782

Plymouth ☎ (01752) 501478

Firing may be cancelled at short notice even after the publication of firing notices. If the red flags are **not** flying by 09.00 from April to September inclusive and by 10.00 from October to March inclusive, then no live firing will take place that day. Any firing or explosions you then hear will be blank cartridges or fireworks.

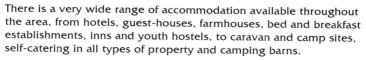

ACCOMMODATION

There is a very wide range of accommodation available throughout the area, from hotels, guest-houses, farmhouses, bed and breakfast establishments, inns and youth hostels, to caravan and camp sites, self-catering in all types of property and camping barns.

HOTELS, GUEST HOUSES, BED AND BREAKFAST, INNS

Details of this type of accommodation can be obtained from the appropriate local Tourist Information Centre. These are listed towards the end of the Fact File.

The Dartmoor Tourist Association issues a comprehensive guide to both serviced and self-catering accommodation in the Dartmoor area, ☎ (01822) 890567 or write to Dartmoor Tourist Association, The Duchy Building, Tavistock Road, Princetown, PL20 6QF.

FARM HOLIDAYS

Cream of West Devon Farm Holiday Group, Helen Alford
☎ (01837) 861381

Farm Holiday Bureau, Linda Harvey ☎ (01626) 833266
West Devon Friendly Farm Holiday Group, Jane Pyle ☎ (01363) 82510

YOUTH HOSTELS

Details of YHA hostels in the area from Youth Hostel Association, 11b, York Road, Salisbury, SP2 7AP. ☎ (01722) 337515. (There are Youth Hostels at Okehampton, Steps Bridge and Bellever).

CARAVAN AND CAMP SITES

Devon County Council produces a leaflet *DEVON Self-catering Holiday Parks, Caravan and Camping* which may be obtained from Devon Tourist Information Centre, Exeter Services, Sidmouth Road, Exeter, EX2 7HF, ☎ (01392) 437581 or e-mail ahopkins@mf.devon-cc.gov.uk or local Tourist Information Centres.

SELF-CATERING

Local Tourist Information Centres and the following agencies will be pleased to supply details of properties available or contact Devon TIC as above:

Dartmoor and South Devon Farm and Country Holidays,
☎ 901364) 621391
Devon Connection, ☎ (01548) 560964 or website
www.devonconnection.co.uk
Helpful Holidays, ☎ (01647) 433593

CAMPING BARNS

There are a number of camping barns on Dartmoor.
For details ☎ (01271) 324420.

SPECIALIST HOLIDAYS

For details of 'Activity Holidays, Learning Holidays and Event Packages' contact Economy and Tourism, Exeter City Council, Civic Centre, Paris Street, Exeter, EX1 1JJ. ☎ (01392) 265900.

'LAST MINUTE' BOOKINGS

Contact the Devon TIC, ☎ (01392) 437581 or e-mail ahopkins@mf.devon-cc.gov.uk. Give details of the location, type and price range of the accommodation being sought and they will try to find what is wanted and make the booking.

DARTMOOR FOR THE DISABLED

Under the heading *Easy-Going Dartmoor* the National Park Authority and Countryside Access Group for Dartmoor have produced a booklet with information on 14 walks specifically designed for disabled or less mobile visitors, or those with babies in prams or young children in push-chairs. The booklet also has information on horse riding centres which cater for the disabled, and the position of toilets for the disabled. Large print copies of the booklet are available for the visually handicapped. Copies may be obtained by telephoning ☎ (01822) 890414.

For further information contact:

Countryside Access Group for Dartmoor,
Parke, Haytor Road, Bovey Tracey, Devon TQ13 9JQ ☎ (01626) 832093

or contact individual organisations:

Riding for the Disabled Association, ☎ (01752) 894348

Devon County Association for the Blind, ☎ (01392) 876666

FOOD

Recommending restaurants is fraught with danger. Much safer is to recommend the publication *Taste of the West: Devon* which lists not only good places to eat, but places where food, including local specialities, can be purchased. It is available from Tourist Information Offices or the main offices of West Country and Devon Tourism.

PUBLIC TRANSPORT

Being largely uninhabited, Dartmoor suffers from a lack of public transport. Buses do follow the roads that bisect the moor, and also visit most of the villages, but these buses are infrequent and the walker will occasionally need to modify a walk or extend it to make use of them.

At the moor's edge the situation is better, particularly at the southern edge where relatively frequent services follow the A38 between Exeter and Plymouth.

A booklet on the public transport options on Dartmoor (buses and trains) is published annually and can be obtained from the moor's Tourist Information Centres or by telephoning: ☎ (01392), (01803) or (01271) 382800.

RECREATION

CANOEING

Heavy winter rain and occasional summer downpours often create challenging canoe courses on the larger Dartmoor rivers. However, there is no public right of navigation on virtually all Britain's non-tidal waterways, and even where rights do exist there is not necessarily a right of access across land to the riverbank. Increasingly such access, if it exists, has been granted only to British Canoe Union members. For information on access to Dartmoor's rivers please contact the Head of Recreation at the National Park Authority or the Local Access Officer of the British Canoe Union.

The National Park Authority has issued a Code of Conduct for canoeists: this is available from National Park Visitor Centres. The leaflet also includes advice on personal safety both in the canoe and in the water should you be unlucky enough to capsize. The latter includes advice on how to avoid infection from water-borne pollutants and diseases.

CLIMBING

Dartmoor's tors are ideal for climbers (particularly those willing to lose skin from their hands as the granite is very rough), though the lack of height of many tors is something of a drawback. Only at Haytor/Low Man and the Dewerstone does the granite gain any real height. However, at other places, particularly Hound Tor and Vixen Tors the short, but steep, tors offer real challenges.

Though the climber would seem to offer little chance of damage to the tors, climbing does pose a threat to the landscape. The indiscriminate use of fixed belays, particular at the top of tors set into, rather than on top of, hillsides, can cause soil erosion, and belaying or abseiling from trees can cause damage to the very few substantial trees on the moor. To counteract these threats the National Park Authority has issued a Code of Conduct for climbers: this is available from National Park Visitor Centres.

A guide to climbing on Dartmoor's tors (and to the cliffs of South Devon) has been published by Cordee.

Please note that climbing is not allowed on all tors – National Park Visitor Centres have lists of accessible tors.

CYCLING

The public roads that cross high Dartmoor are ideal for cycling for although the moor is an upland area, it is a relatively flat plateau with limited climbs. Cyclists are also allowed on public bridleways and byways, on most Forestry Commission roads and certain cycle tracks. The latter include the Plym Valley Cycle Way and the trackbed of the disused.

Princetown railway. The National Park Authority is continuously seeking to improve access for cyclists on other routes.

However, there is no legal right of way for cyclists on public footpaths or on open moorland. The Dartmoor Commons Act, 1985 allows access on foot or on horseback, but not on a cycle. Off-road cycling (mountain biking) has become increasingly popular in recent years, but indiscriminate riding has antagonised landowners, walkers and horseriders. Fast cycling over soft moorland can cause considerable damage and should be avoided at all times. The National Park Authority has issued a Code of Conduct for cyclists: this is available from National Park Visitor Centres. The intention of the code is to maximise enjoyment for cyclists while avoiding problems with local landowners and other moorland users, and damage to the landscape.

The National Park Authority also issues a series of leaflets – *Off Road Cycling with Moor Care and Less Wear* – with details of permitted routes.

There are a number of cycle hire shops on or close to the moor. Ask at the local Tourist Information Centre for details.

FISHING

Dartmoor's eight reservoirs are controlled by South West Water who maintain fish stocks and regulate fishing. Information on the type of fish (rainbow or brown trout) at each reservoir and the permits required to fish them can be obtained from South West Water ☎ (01837) 871565. Leaflets are also available at local Information Offices.

Below: Round Pound
Opposite page; Top: Haytor Granite Tramway Bottom: Haytor

GOLF

There are golf courses at:

Ashbury GC, Okehampton,	☎ 01837 55453
Hurdwick GC, Butcher Hill, Tavistock,	☎ 01822 612746
Manor House Hotel, Moretonhampstead,	☎ 01647 440355
Newton Abbot GC, Stover, nr Bovey Tracey,	☎ 01626 52460
Okehampton GC, Tors Road, Okehampton,	☎ 01837 52113
Tavistock GC, Down Road, Tavistock,	☎ 01822 612049
Teign Valley GC, Nr Bovey Tracey,	☎ 01647 253026
Wrangton GC, South Brent,	☎ 01364 73229
Yelverton GC, Yelverton,	☎ 01822 852824

HORSE RIDING

Horse riding can be enjoyed on open moorland – the Dartmoor Commons Act, 1985 ensured open access to common land for those on horseback as well as those on foot – public bridleways, byways and certain permitted routes, ie. where landowners have given permission for riders to cross their land.

Riding can cause erosion of the moor in the same way as walking: there may be fewer riders, but a single horse can cause much more damage than a single walker, especially if ridden fast over soft ground. The National Park Authority publishes a Code of Conduct for riders: this is available from National Park Visitor Centres. The leaflet also gives tips on safety for riders. The extensive warrening of some areas of Dartmoor means that riders are at risk from rabbit holes. As a result, it is recommended that crash helmets are worn.

There are many horse riding stables on or close to the moor. Ask at the local Tourist Information Centre for details.

LEISURE CENTRES

There are leisure centres at:

South Hams Centre, Ivybridge,	☎ (01752) 896999
Simmons Park, Okehampton,	☎ (01837) 52073
Meadowlands, The Wharf, Tavistock,	☎ (01822) 617774

as well as at the nearby big cities of Exeter and Plymouth.

LETTERBOXING

The name letterbox came from the early use of the box at Cranmere Pool: a walker would bring a self-addressed card to the pool and exchange it for the one left by the last visitor, posting that on his return to 'civilisation'. The recipient would then marvel (or not) at the time taken for his card to reach him.

Cranmere Pool was Dartmoor's first letterbox, but further boxes were placed at Ducks Pool in 1938 and Fur Tor in 1951 (there was already another at Taw marsh, put there in 1894). All these locations are relatively inaccessible, a degree of commitment being required to reach them (though the military road on the northern moor has now made Cranmere Pool much easier to reach). In time many more letterboxes were added, groups growing up who used the placing and finding of the boxes to enhance their enjoyment of the moor.

It is thought that at one time there were as many as 1,500 letterboxes on the moor. Such a number gave the National Park Authority cause for concern: many of the boxes were deliberately hidden, the hiding and the subsequent searching by other letterboxers damaging wildlife habitats. As a result, a Code of Practice has been published (a leaflet on letterboxing, including the Code of Practice, is available from Visitor Centres) which defines the type of letterbox which can be used, where it should be sited and, most importantly, the 'no go' areas for boxes.

Today letterboxing is a semi-organised sport under the direction of the Dartmoor 100 Club. Authorised boxes have visitor's books which letterboxers stamp with their own stamps, and stamps which the letterboxer uses to stamp his/her record sheet. Collectors of 100 stamps can join the club.

SWIMMING POOLS

There are outdoor swimming pools at Ashburton, Bovey Tracey, Buckfastleigh, Chagford and Moretonhampstead.

There are indoor pools at Ivybridge (South Hams Leisure Centre), Okehampton (Simmons Park) and Tavistock (Meadowlands), and at Newton Abbot and Paignton as well as at Exeter and Plymouth.

WALKING

Walking is by far the most popular way of exploring Dartmoor. Access to the common land, together with a further 372 miles (600km) of rights of way within the National Park and additional permissive paths (along which landowners have given permission for walkers to cross their land) allow almost unlimited possibilities. A leaflet published by the National Park Authority gives a Code of Conduct for walkers on the moor. This covers not only personal safety – poor weather, including mists, can occur quickly, disorientating the walker – but certain requests. Chief of these is for dog owners to control their dogs so that grazing animals and wildlife are not disturbed. This is particularly important during the spring when moorland birds are nesting, and grazing animals are giving birth. Walkers are also asked to follow existing paths to avoid erosion and, where possible, to follow hard tracks.

On the northern moor there are a number of peat passes cut through the blanket bog which should be used to minimise erosion of the bog. The passes were cut by Frank Phillpotts, a Victorian gentleman, to help moormen, but chiefly hunters, to travel more easily across difficult sections of the moor. Phillpotts cut down through the peat to the granite sub-strata, creating a good path for horses. His half-dozen or so passes are all marked – at each end – by memorial stones/plaques erected by his brother and son.

Dartmoor is touched by two long distance footpaths, each of them 'unofficial' in the sense that they are not National Trails. The Two Moors Way was created by Devon County Council and the Devon Ramblers Association. It starts (or ends) at Ivybridge, crossing Ugborough Moor and Huntingdon Warren to reach Holne. It then heads north, crossing Hamel

Down to Grimspound, then bearing west to Bennet's Cross before skirting the northern moor via Chagford, the Teign Gorge and Drewsteignton. The route then continues north, eventually crossing Exmoor to reach the sea.

The Tarka Trail is also a Devon County Council route. The route is a figure-of-eight including a section of the North Devon Coastal Path. On Dartmoor the route links Okehampton to Belstone, follows the River Taw through Belstone Cleave to Sticklepath, then heads north-east to South Tawton before heading north out the National Park.

Walkers on the long distance footpaths who are back-packing, that is carrying tents, sleeping bags and food should acquire a copy of the Dartmoor Commons Bylaws. These prohibit camping within 100yd (90m) of a road or prohibited area and the lighting of fires. The areas where camping is prohibited are marked on a leaflet obtainable from Visitor Centres.

For those walkers who do not feel they have the necessary experience to tackle the open moor, or who would like to know more about the history or wildlife of certain areas, an extensive walks programme of guided walks is organised each year. Details of the dates, start times and routes of these walks are published in the *Dartmoor Visitor*, a free newspaper available at National Park Visitor Centres.

Although some walks are suggested in the book, no detailed route descriptions are given. Those wishing to walk the moor could do worse than obtain a copy of the present author's book: *Collins' Ramblers Guide: Dartmoor* by Richard Sale (published by Harper Collins 2000).

TRANSPORT

BY CAR

M4/M5 or M25/M3/A303/A30 to Exeter. A38 Devon Expressway links Exeter to Plymouth with access to all destinations in between.

BY RAIL

Direct services from London (Paddington), the Midlands, North of England, South Wales and Scotland. Contact National Rail Enquiry Office ☎ (0345) 484950 for further details or website, www.rail.co.uk/ukrail/home.htm

BY COACH

National Express runs regular services to South Devon from most areas of Britain. ☎ (0990) 808080 for details or website, http://www.eurolines.co.uk

BY AIR

Direct flights to Plymouth from Cork, Jersey, Guernsey, Paris and London Gatwick. Connecting flights from other UK destinations. Contact British Airways for further details, ☎ (0345) 222111 or website, www.british-airways.co.uk

BY SEA

To Plymouth from Roscoff, Brittany and Santander, Spain. Contact Brittany Ferries, ☎ (0990) 360360 (Plymouth); ☎ (298) 292800 (Roscoff); ☎ (942) 220000 (Santander) or website, www.brittany-ferries.co.uk/home.htm

TOURIST INFORMATION CENTRES

NATIONAL PARK INFORMATION CENTRES

Lower Car Park on the main road near Haytor,   ☎ (01364) 661520
Riverside Car Park at Newbridge,   ☎ (01364) 631303
Car Park at Postbridge,   ☎ (018220 880272
High Moorland Visitor Centre, Tavistock Road, Princetown,
   ☎ (01822) 890414

OTHER INFORMATION CENTRES

Town Hall, Ashburton,   ☎ (01364) 653426
Station Road, Bovey Tracey,   ☎ (01626) 832047
Leonard's Road, Ivybridge,   ☎ (01752) 897035
*The Square, Moretonhampstead,   ☎ (01647) 440043
*White Hart Courtyard (adjacent to the Museum), Okehampton,
   ☎ (01837) 53020
Island House, 9 The Barbican, Plymouth,   ☎ (01752) 264849
*Town Hall, Bedford Square, Tavistock,   ☎ (01822) 612938

*open in summer season only

WEATHER

The high moorland plateau of Dartmoor intercepts the prevailing south-westerly winds that reach Britain from the Atlantic laden with moisture from their sweep across the ocean. The plateau forces the air to rise and cool, causing clouds to form and rain to fall more often than in surrounding areas. But don't be put off – on good days Dartmoor is glorious, and all that rain goes to make it what it is. However, just in case, a weather forecast for the moor (as well as Exmoor and the remainder of the South-West Peninsula) is available by ringing ☎ (0891) 141203. The forecast covers the next 48 – 72 hours and is updated daily at 7am and 7pm.

LANDMARK
VISITORS GUIDES

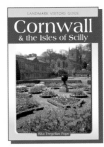

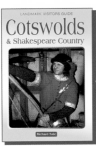

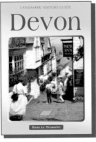

Cornwall
ISBN: 1 901522 09 1
256pp, Full colour
£9.95

Cotswolds
ISBN: 1 901522 12 1
224pp, Full colour
£9.99

Devon
ISBN: 1 901522 42 3
224pp, Full colour
£9.95

Dorset
ISBN: 1 901522 46 6
240pp, Full colour
£9.95

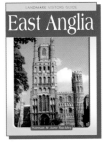

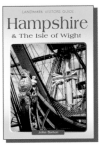

East Anglia
ISBN: 1 901522 58 X
224pp, Full colour
£9.95

Guernsey
ISBN: 1 901522 48 2
224pp, Full colour
£9.95

Hampshire
ISBN: 1 901522 14 8
224pp, Full colour
£9.95

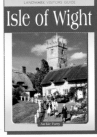

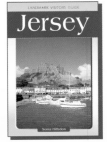

Harrogate
ISBN: 1 901522 55 5
96pp, Full colour
£4.95

Hereford
ISBN: 1 901522 72 5
96pp, Full colour
£5.95

Isle of Wight
ISBN: 1 901522 71 7
96pp, Full colour
£5.95

Jersey
ISBN: 1 901522 47 4
224pp, Full colour
£9.99

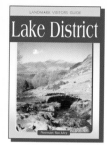

Lake District
ISBN: 1 901522 38 5
224pp, Full colour
£9.95

New Forest
ISBN: 1 901522 70 9
96pp, Full colour
£5.95

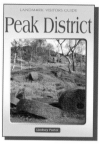

Peak District
ISBN: 1 901522 25 3
240pp, Full colour
£9.99

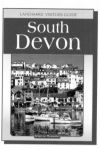

South Devon
ISBN: 1 901522 52 0
96pp, Full colour
£5.95

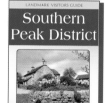

Southern Peak
ISBN: 1 901522 27 X
96pp, Full colour
£5.95

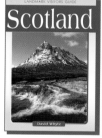

Scotland
ISBN: 1 901522 18 0
288pp, Full colour
£11.95

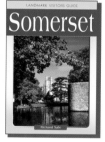

Somerset
ISBN: 1 901522 40 7
224pp, Full colour
£10.95

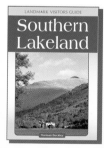

Southern Lakeland
ISBN: 1 901522 53 9
96pp, Full colour
£5.95

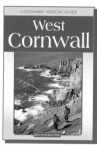

West Cornwall
ISBN: 1 901522 24 5
96pp, Full colour
£5.95

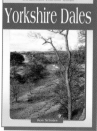

Yorkshire Dales
ISBN: 1 901522 41 5
224pp, Full colour
£9.95

Pack
2 months
into
2 weeks
with your
Landmark
Visitors
Guides

INDEX

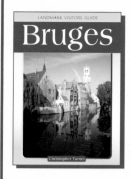
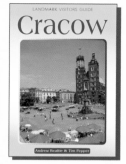

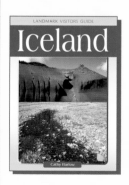
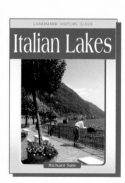
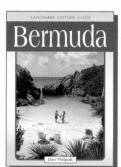

Published by
Landmark Publishing Ltd,
Waterloo House, 12 Compton, Ashbourne, Derbyshire DE6 1DA England
Tel: (01335) 347349 Fax: (01335) 347303 e-mail: landmark@clara.net

1st Edition
ISBN 1 901 522 69 5

British Library Cataloguing in Publication Data: a catalogue record for this book
is available from the British Library.

Print: Gutenberg Press Ltd, Malta
Designed by: James Allsopp

Front cover: The village of Widecombe-in-the-Moor
Back cover, top: The rock basin on Kes Tor
Back cover, bottom: Powder Mill's
Page 1: Clapper Bridge, Wallabrook

Picture Credits
Lindsey Porter: Front cover, Back cover, bottom, p3, p4, p8, p9T, p21,
p22, p23, p24, p27T, p28, p32, p38, p40, p41, p44, p48, p50,
p51, p54, p55, p57, p63, p69, p73, p75, p87

Canonteign Falls & Lakeland: p34

All other photographs are supplied by Richard Sale